DEVELOPING SELF-ESTEEM:
A Guide for Positive Success

REVISED EDITION

Connie D. Palladino, Ph.D.

A FIFTY-MINUTE™ SERIES BOOK

CRISP PUBLICATIONS, INC.
Menlo Park, California

DEVELOPING SELF-ESTEEM:
A Guide for Positive Success

REVISED EDITION

Connie D. Palladino, Ph.D.

CREDITS:
Editor: **Michael Crisp**
Layout and Composition: **Interface Studio**
Cover Design: **Carol Harris**
Artwork: **Ralph Mapson**

Copyright © 1989, 1994 by Crisp Publications, Inc.
Printed in the United States of America

English language Crisp books are distributed worldwide. Our major international distributors include:

CANADA: Reid Publishing Ltd., Box 69559—109 Thomas St., Oakville, Ontario, Canada L6J 7R4. TEL: (905) 842-4428, FAX: (905) 842-9327

Raincoast Books Distribution Ltd., 112 East 3rd Avenue, Vancouver, British Columbia, Canada V5T 1C8. TEL: (604) 873-6581, FAX: (604) 874-2711

AUSTRALIA: Career Builders, P.O. Box 1051, Springwood, Brisbane, Queensland, Australia 4127. TEL: 841-1061, FAX: 841-1580

NEW ZEALAND: Career Builders, P.O. Box 571, Manurewa, Auckland, New Zealand. TEL: 266-5276, FAX: 266-4152

JAPAN: Phoenix Associates Co., Mizuho Bldg. 2-12-2, Kami Osaki, Shinagawa-Ku, Tokyo 141, Japan. TEL: 3-443-7231, FAX: 3-443-7640

Selected Crisp titles are also available in other languages. Contact International Rights Manager Suzanne Kelly at (415) 323-6100 for more information.

Library of Congress Catalog Card Number 93-074054
Palladino, Connie D.
ISBN 1-56052-261-5

This book is printed on recyclable paper with soy ink.

INTRODUCTION

Have you ever found yourself saying, ''I can't do that,'' or wondering why you don't feel successful? Do you often wonder who you really are, where you are going or what your real life's purpose is? If any of these reflect your thoughts, this book should help you.

Unfortunately, too many people, regardless of their age, income or education, worry about failure, doubt their strengths, feel unfocused and insecure, are overly self-critical and stop short of getting what they want in life. Why? Because of poor self-esteem, which ends up affecting everything they do, think or say.

As a professional development consultant, I have observed that a significant percentage of career and personal problems are directly related to a person's self-esteem. Consequently, the focus of my work (and the information in this book) has been developed to assist others to better understand who they are. Once a person's overall strengths have been identified and accepted, that individual can then take responsibility for his or her actions and gain a sense of direction, increased confidence and improved feelings of self-esteem.

One thing is for sure—PEOPLE WHO FEEL GOOD ABOUT THEMSELVES PRODUCE POSITIVE RESULTS. Good luck as you complete the exercises and activities in this book.

Connie Palladino

Connie D. Palladino

ACKNOWLEDGMENTS

The author would like to acknowledge and thank the following individuals for their thoughtful and helpful review.

Kenneth Woodrow, M.D.
Menlo Park, Ca.

Sherry Herrgott, M.A.
Educational Consultant
Sunnyvale, Ca.

Pat Lemp Millar, Ph.D.
Millar and Associates
Los Altos, Ca.

Lynn Silton, M.A.
Project Management Consultant
Member of the California State Task Force to Promote Self-Esteem, and Personal and Social Responsibility
Palo Alto, Ca.

DEDICATION

A special tribute to you, Mom and Dad, on your 50th anniversary this year. Thank you for your confidence, faith, love and direction. You both have served as true role models by providing a nurturing, supportive environment for my personal growth.

I LOVE YOU

ABOUT THIS BOOK

This practical and realistic workbook is designed to inspire you to try new techniques and ideas. If you practice the suggested exercises and carefully read the material, you can enhance your success and improve your self-esteem, both at work and in your personal life. Self-esteem is a personal trait that can be improved by any person willing to commit him- or herself to the task of positive self-development. The concepts and exercises in this book have been completed by hundreds of individuals in a workshop titled ''Believe in Yourself and Make it Happen.'' Their feedback and insights are included in this book. The result is a practical and realistic approach to building better self-esteem.

As you are introduced to the self-esteem process described in the following pages, you will learn:

☐ **WHAT SELF-ESTEEM IS.**

☐ **HOW TO BEGIN TO RISK CHANGE AND OVERCOME FEAR.**

☐ **HOW TO CREATE A POSITIVE BELIEF SYSTEM AT HOME AND AT WORK.**

☐ **HOW TO IDENTIFY YOUR UNIQUE STRENGTHS.**

☐ **HOW TO IDENTIFY WHAT YOU WANT.**

☐ **HOW TO TAKE RESPONSIBILITY FOR WHAT YOU WANT.**

Self-esteem is the bridge between who you are and what you do. A person with high self-esteem has learned what is important in life. An individual with high self-esteem will not get distracted by feelings of guilt, fear or self-doubt. With high self-esteem a person can make choices without compromising values or ethics and take responsibility for his or her actions.

ABOUT THE AUTHOR

Dr. Palladino is a former teacher who worked in the hotel-management and high-technology fields before deciding to redirect her life by going into career counseling in 1977. She holds her Ph.D. in Educational Psychology and her M.A. in Marriage and Family Counseling. She is also a National Certified Career Counselor. Dr. Palladino is the author of *Focus: A Professional Development Program, Developing Self-Esteem* (translated into 6 languages), *The Self Esteem Styles Inventory and Guide* (Palladino and Silton) and *Believe in Yourself and Make It Happen* audio tape. She presently teaches at the University of San Francisco and the Career Action Center in Palo Alto.

CONTENTS

CONTENTS (continued)

P A R T

I

HOW TO BELIEVE IN YOURSELF
AND OTHERS

WHAT IS SELF-ESTEEM?

RISK CHANGE AND OVERCOME FEAR

**CREATE A POSITIVE BELIEF SYSTEM
AT WORK AND AT HOME**

SECTION ONE

WHAT IS SELF-ESTEEM?

> *"Self-esteem is appreciating one's own worth and importance, and having the character to be accountable for oneself and to act responsibly toward others."*
>
> California State Task Force to Promote Self-Esteem, and Personal and Social Responsibility

> *"A confidence and satisfaction in oneself"*
>
> Webster's Dictionary

Self-esteem is a state of mind. It is the way you feel and think about yourself and others; and it is measured by the way you act. Your self-esteem serves as the bridge between who you are and what you do. It can also be defined as your internal belief system and how you experience life externally. High self-esteem is the most positive phrase in the English language. It relates to having a positive sense of your inherent worth as a person. Self-esteem is made up of learned feelings and positive thoughts that reflect a positive attitude of "I CAN DO IT" versus a pessimistic attitude of "I CAN'T DO IT."

Self-esteem is self-confidence, self-worth and self-respect. It involves respecting others, as well as feeling a sense of harmony and peace within yourself.

The key to elevated self-esteem is the willingness to take responsibility for your feelings, desires, thoughts, abilities and interests and to accept your overall strengths and act accordingly.

Your self-esteem affects everything you do. It reflects "you" to everyone with whom you come in contact. Each of us is born with the capacity for positive feelings, but it is possible to learn not to like yourself through practice and/or life experiences. This book will teach you to appreciate your self-worth and importance.

Feeling good about yourself is not a luxury; it is an absolute necessity.

WHAT IS SELF-ESTEEM? (continued)

Self-esteem is not a fixed or rigid state. It changes depending on what you experience or how you are feeling.

Most low self-esteem is caused by negative emotional reactions. It is not easy to reach adulthood with a sense of high self-worth today, because of the many factors that come into play in this complex world. Unfortunate childhood experiences, criticism from adults, peers, your environment, media, cultural backgrounds or society in general can cause feelings of inferiority and low self-esteem. If these feelings are reinforced by negative belief patterns, they can become habit-forming, and low self-esteem can become the norm for an individual.

As you become an adult, you depend on others for a sense of importance. Negative feelings and thinking patterns can become powerful illusions of truth. Physical, emotional and psychological consequences will influence your thinking, and your mind can form value judgments.

Self-esteem is both conscious and unconscious. It is an ongoing evaluation of yourself, a belief about what you can and cannot do. Self-esteem *can* be learned, but it does not happen overnight or by chance.

A new decision and a new life are possible. "The miracles come from within. You are not that unloved child anymore. You can be reborn, rejecting the old messages and their consequent diseases. When you choose to love you will have days when you're not all you'd like to be, but you *can* learn to forgive yourself. You cannot change your shortcomings until you accept yourself despite them."

Bernie Siegel

Self-Esteem can be learned, so let's begin to learn how.

HOW WOULD *YOU* DEFINE SELF-ESTEEM?

Check any box you feel helps define what self-esteem means to you.

For me, self-esteem means:

☐ Believing in myself and my self-worth.

☐ The ability to see my place in the world realistically and optimistically.

☐ A confidence in my abilities to make changes and meet life's challenges head-on.

☐ A capacity for understanding my character weaknesses and working toward self-improvement of specific weaknesses.

☐ A knowledge of self and acceptance of that knowledge.

☐ The ability to recognize my individual uniqueness and take pride in things that make "me" unique.

☐ A belief in my self-worth. A healthy admiration of my abilities.

☐ A belief in what I can do. A positive outlook and confidence to try something new.

☐ The ability to assess and apply my skills in a positive and optimistic manner.

☐ Understanding that I am of value to myself and others, regardless of the situation.

☐ Knowing who I am, what I can do, and how to project this knowledge.

☐ A love of self, regardless of any specific performance.

☐ Liking myself, respecting myself and being willing to risk and fail at things.

☐ Accepting who I am and having the courage and strength to design my life the way I want it to be.

Author's note: All of the above are acceptable definitions of self-esteem. Most people would check several boxes.

IS SELF-ESTEEM RELATED TO YOUR FEELINGS OF SUCCESS?

How successful do you perceive yourself? Are your thoughts consistent with your actions? What aspects of your life need special attention?

INSTRUCTIONS:

Place the number that best describes how you perceive yourself at work in the space provided. Then repeat the exercise by how you perceive yourself away from work. (Disregard the letters in parentheses following each question.)

Scale: Very High = 5
Moderately High = 4
Average = 3
Moderately Low = 2
Very Low = 1

PERSONAL AND WORK EVALUATION REVIEW

AT WORK	AWAY FROM WORK		
3	____	1.	I feel successful in my present work/career. (D)
____	____	2.	I feel satisfied with my present work/career path. (D)
____	____	3.	I consider myself to be a risk taker. (H)
5	5	4.	I feel that continuing my education is important. (L)
____	____	5.	I consciously look for the good in others. (B)
____	____	6.	I can do most everything I put my mind to. (B)
____	____	7.	I am comfortable in new social situations. (E)
____	____	8.	I appreciate compliments from others. (E)
____	____	9.	I feel comfortable speaking in front of others. (K)
____	____	10.	I enjoy telling others of my successes. (A)
____	____	11.	I am an optimistic person. (B)
____	____	12.	I am goal-oriented. (I)
____	____	13.	I am comfortable making most decisions. (G)
____	____	14.	I am in good physical condition. (C)
____	____	15.	I am respected by others for who I am. (A)

AT WORK	AWAY FROM WORK		
——	——	16.	I project a positive self-image. (J)
——	——	17.	I am an active listener. (P)
——	——	18.	I like being responsible for projects and others. (P)
——	——	19.	I enjoy controversial discussions. (O)
——	——	20.	I find obstacles challenging. (H)
——	——	21.	I am able to ask for help without feeling guilty. (F)
——	——	22.	I can laugh at my mistakes. (H)
——	——	23.	I am responsible for my thoughts and actions. (F)
——	——	24.	I am direct when I voice my feelings. (F)
——	——	25.	I am leading a balanced life. (M)
——	——	26.	I am an enthusiastic person. (B)
——	——	27.	I use direct eye contact when talking to others. (N)
——	——	28.	I genuinely like myself for who I am. (A)
——	——	29.	I exercise daily. (C)
5	4	30.	I feel it is important to dress for success. (J)

Add up your points and place your total in the box provided.

TOTAL POINTS: ☐ **AT WORK**

☐ **AWAY FROM WORK**

SCALE

(120–150) = **Very High Self-Esteem**
(90–119) = **Moderately High Self-Esteem**
(89–60) = **Average Self-Esteem**
(31–59) = **Moderately Low Self-Esteem**
(0–30) = **Low Self-Esteem**

Before continuing, REVIEW your answers so you will be better prepared to answer the questions in the exercise on the next page.

PERSONAL AND WORK EVALUATION SUMMARY

INSTRUCTIONS:

Review the exercise you just completed (pages 6 and 7) and place an "X" next to each letter that you feel needs some work. Refer to the letters in parentheses following each question to complete this exercise.

AT WORK	AWAY FROM WORK		
X	X	A.	Overall level of self-esteem
X	X	B.	Positive mental attitude
X	X	C.	Physical exercise program
X	X	D.	Career focus/direction
___	___	E.	Social/interpersonal skills
X	X	F.	Assertiveness Training
X	X	G.	Decision making
X	X	H.	Risk taking/overcoming fear
X	X	I.	Goal-setting strategies
X	X	J.	Personal appearance/self-image
X	X	K.	Public speaking training
___	___	L.	Professional skills training
X	X	M.	Balanced personal and work life
___	___	N.	Awareness of nonverbal messages
X	X	O.	Negotiation skills
X	X	P.	Leadership/management training

Review the above list before proceeding to the next exercise.

INSTRUCTIONS:

Using the information from the exercise on page 8, prioritize what you feel needs immediate attention from the PERSONAL and WORK EVALUATION SUMMARY. Select no fewer than three and no more than six areas you want to improve.

IMMEDIATE ATTENTION

My priorities are:

1. _Positive Mental attitudes_

2. _Risk Taking / Overcoming Fear_

3. _Physical Exercise Prog._

4. _Goal Setting Strategies_

5. _Leadership Training_

6. _Public Speaking Training_

That which is not written down becomes lost and vague. Success can occur in your life, but awareness is the first key.

WHO WEARS WHAT MASK?

Low self-esteem can destroy a person's ability to think, feel or act in a positive way. Hiding behind a ''mask'' may become a common way to cover up true feelings. The result of wearing a mask to fool others often results in guilt, fear, anger, emptiness, loneliness or depression. You need to be able to identify which mask you wear, recognize those masks other people wear and emphasize the need to trust what we have inside (self-esteem) rather than depend on external affirmation (other-esteem).

INSTRUCTIONS:	Think about people with whom you relate daily.
	List (first names only) anyone who wears the following masks. Include yourself when appropriate.

1. The Workaholic: A person who runs from task to task, unable to rest. One who constantly seeks greater financial gains, higher positions or respect and admiration from others but who is rarely satisfied with what he or she has.

Names: 1. _Chere_ 2. _Mike_ 3. _____

2. The Nice Guy/Gal: He/she is always there with a shoulder to cry on, to offer a helping hand or to become the problem solver. This person may be caring for others out of need to be accepted. He/she may put far too much energy into relationships that can drain or delete his/her energy or lower one's self-esteem.

Names: 1. _Myself_ 2. _____ 3. _____

3. The Poor Me: A person who constantly talks about problems, poor health or negative family and work issues. He/she needs to draw attention to unpleasant events in order to get attention.

Names: 1. _Mommy_ 2. _Michele_ 3. _____

4. The Trouble Maker: A person you can depend on to disagree with you about most everything. This person wants to be liked, but the result is self-destructive.

Names: 1. _____ 2. _____ 3. _____

5. The Perfectionist: A person who is always striving to be the best, to attain excellence in all that he/she does. One who is involved in constant comparison with others.

Names: 1. _Roger_ 2. _____ 3. _____

6. Other Masks: People who are always feeling tired or sick or who have a weak handshake and indirect eye contact. People who constantly feel depressed, anxious or withdrawn. People who are easily angered or always seem to project a negative attitude.

Names: 1. _____ 2. _____ 3. _____

If you recognize a mask that you wear or can now identify ones that others wear, you have a good starting point for understanding how to build improved self-esteem.

LOW SELF-ESTEEM? WHY?

As babies most of us were told how cute and adorable we were. Families and friends made us the center of everyone's attention. Unfortunately, this attention did not last and as we became adults we found ourselves questioning the love and attention we once felt.

Why? Is it because of how we perceive ourselves physically, mentally or emotionally compared to others; our race or ethnic group; the messages we hear from our business colleagues, parents or friends? Or is it the way we think others perceive us?

_____

_____

_____

_____

The truth is we all hear those negative messages echoing in our ears at one time or another. What we need to do is prevent those sounds from dominating our feelings and behavior, which ultimately effect our entire life.

TAKE A BREAK — EMPTY THE SOUNDS

List five negative messages that you remember hearing as a child or messages that you hear today.

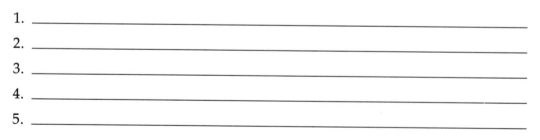

e.g., "I am going to fail in my new business."

1. _____
2. _____
3. _____
4. _____
5. _____

Now take these same five negative statements and turn them into positive ones.

RULES TO REMEMBER

- Put the statement in the first person: "I or My."
- Use the present tense.
- State what you **want**, not what you don't want; e.g., "I am a success in my new business today."

Positive Statements

1. _I want to be a *good* educator_
2. _I want to be able to speak Spanish fluently_
3. _I want to be able to read & write Spanish proficiently_
4. _I want to learn how to speak French_
5. _I want to be a success in all those thgs_

Put all five statements on 3 by 5 cards and repeat daily. Reinforce what you **want**, not what you don't want. Create positive energy in your life and maintain your feelings of self-esteem.

(Turn the page and review your high self-esteem.)

HOW HIGH IS YOUR SELF-ESTEEM?

_____ 1. I feel my work/career has progressed more because of luck than because I deserve it.

_____ 2. I often find myself thinking, ''Why can't I be more successful?''

_____ 3. I do not believe I am working up to my potential.

_____ 4. I consider it a failure when I do not accomplish my goals.

_____ 5. When others are nice to me, I often feel suspicious.

_____ 6. Giving others compliments about their strengths often makes me feel uncomfortable.

_____ 7. It is difficult to see co-workers promoted because I often feel I am more deserving.

_____ 8. I do not necessarily believe that our minds have a direct influence on our physical well-being.

_____ 9. When things are going well, this usually will not last for me.

_____ 10. I place a high value on what others think of me.

_____ 11. I like to impress my supervisor.

_____ 12. I find it difficult to face up to my mistakes.

_____ 13. I am not always comfortable saying what I mean.

_____ 14. I find it hard to say I am sorry.

_____ 15. I tend to accept change in my job slowly because of fear.

_____ 16. Procrastination is a good word to describe my work habits.

_____ 17. I often find myself thinking, "Why even try? I won't make it."

_____ 18. When my boss praises me, I usually do not believe him or her.

_____ 19. I do not think my co-workers want me to advance professionally.

_____ 20. I avoid people who I think do not like me.

_____ 21. My attitude toward life could improve.

_____ 22. I tend to blame my parents for how my life is turning out.

_____ 23. I find it difficult to look for the good in others.

_____ 24. I do not think people can change their attitudes.

_____ 25. I really do not believe that a self-help book will make a difference in one's self-esteem.

Add up all your TRUE and FALSE statements.

TRUE: _____ **FALSE:** _____

If you scored over half of the items TRUE, you may want to spend some quality time with yourself, or with a counselor, thinking about your life. Think about why you have these feelings.

If the majority of your answers were FALSE, you seem to have good self-esteem and are on your way to greater success and satisfaction.

ATTITUDE IS THE KEY AND INNER SUCCESS IS THE FIRST STEP TO OUTER SUCCESS.

Developing Self-Esteem

YOU ARE UNIQUE . . .

INSTRUCTIONS:

Before you begin to explore your self-esteem, please THINK about and ANSWER the following questions. Write down your intial impressions or thoughts. It is important to be honest in your answers.

1. Write three positive words that describe you.

   (1) _____ (2) _____ (3) _____

2. What single factor contributes most to your self-esteem?

   _____
   _____
   _____

3. What do you consider to be your greatest accomplishment?

   _____
   _____
   _____

4. What would your best friend say is your most positive attribute?

   _____
   _____
   _____

5. What was the most positive message your parents gave you?

   _____
   _____
   _____

6. What would you most like to be remembered for in your life?

   _____
   _____
   _____

7. Circle the words that you believe *best* describe your character, talents and appearance.

talented	motivated	humorous	outgoing
creative	responsible	organized	reserved
caring	professional	understanding	athletic
mature	technical	attractive	a leader

8. List briefly what you are most proud of:

- a difficult job _____
- a goal you reached _____
- an award you received _____
- a compliment you gave _____
- a habit you changed _____

SUMMARY

"You can always better your best and if at first you do not succeed, try another way."

Self-esteem is the bridge between who you are and what you do, the bridge between internal and external success. We all need to recognize that the decisions we make about ourselves when we are young need to be re-evaluated from time to time. Then we can begin the process of acting in new ways.

In order to produce positive results, one needs to focus his/her energy by letting go of unwarranted negative images that may be self-imposed, and turn those negative patterns into positive energy.

The successful individual today has meaningful goals and enjoys the process of getting there. This person continually reassesses who she or he is without feelings of guilt, fear or self-doubt and is able to move through life with a sense of purpose.

Section One was devoted to self-awareness. *Self-awareness* is the first step to any conscious change. The second step is *making a decision to change.* The final step is *taking action.* These next two steps will be covered in the remaining sections of this book.

No one else will ever be you or have your unique combined strengths: physical appearance, skills, accomplishments, personality, interests, thoughts and feelings. Appreciating and accepting your good points and learning how to love yourself does not mean that you are self-centered, egotistical or conceited. Before you can thoroughly give to others, you need to value, appreciate and love yourself.

"When you let go of changing others and work on changing yourself, your outward conditions change."

SECTION TWO

RISK CHANGE AND OVERCOME FEAR

''Change occurs when we take responsibility for our own thoughts, decisions and actions.''

C. Palladino

''You wouldn't worry so much about what other people thought if you realized how seldom they do.''

Eleanor Roosevelt

WHAT IS INVOLVED IN CHANGE?

The truth is, you cannot change or control anyone but yourself. Each person must decide individually whether or not to change. When you learn to spend time working on changing yourself instead of worrying about changing others, you will have made an important discovery.

CHANGE is HARD WORK. It takes EFFORT. Change can cause pain, fear, anger and frustration. Producing it may also mean upsetting balance in a relationship or even letting go of a person who is not supportive of your change. However, change can also lead to an exploration of new goals and energy, which results in a new vision. Although change sometimes leads to failure, if an individual can learn from the experience, his/her courage to try again will be strengthened. Subsequent successes will provide a new vitality and a sense of accomplishment for the individual.

**BEFORE LEARNING HOW TO CHANGE,
PLEASE ANSWER THE FOLLOWING:**

- **Are you open to change?**

- **Are you willing to complete the work that is involved in change?**

- **Are you prepared to experience discomfort that may come with personal change?**

- **Are you willing to try again if you fail?**

If you answered **YES** to these questions this book should help you. Change does not occur overnight, but if you work hard and do not give up, you can make significant, positive changes in your life.

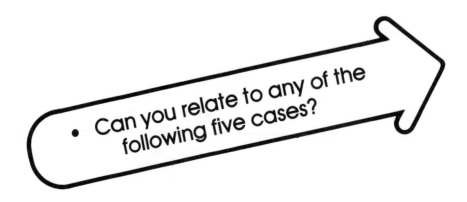

- Can you relate to any of the following five cases?

CASE 1

PEOPLE CHANGE WHEN THERE IS SUCH PAIN OR LOSS THAT THEY SEE NO OTHER WAY OUT.

Sue, a 35-year-old sales representative in the computer supplies industry, was working for a start-up company. She had been separated from her husband for six months. She expressed feelings of depression and was very unhappy with her present job. Sue told a counselor:

''My marriage is a shambles, I hate my sales job and I feel extremely isolated and alone in this city. I feel like I have an emotional block. I cannot make the simplest decision or act to help myself.''

With help, Sue was able to take time to deal with her stressful situation. With the help of a counselor, she was able to identify her marketable strengths and take responsibility for her decisions and actions. Two years later, Sue was happy in her job and able to set some specific goals for her career. She had learned that she was responsible for the direction of her life and took positive action.

COMMENTS: (In the space provided, write any similarities to situations you have personally experienced).

CASE 2

WHEN OLD PATTERNS AND BEHAVIORS NO LONGER WORK

Bill, a 31-year-old, single male is a college graduate. His working experience includes laboratory assistant, store manager, sales representative, business consultant and clerk. Bill is currently unemployed. He recently visited a career counselor and said:

''I've had five jobs in the last eight years. I can't seem to stay interested in any of them. After awhile, I simply quit. Then, I feel frustrated and find myself procrastinating when it comes to looking for another job. I feel like giving up. Why can't I be successful like my father, who is a sales manager?

Bill received not only career counseling, but also psychological counseling. He took a series of interest inventories that indicated he would enjoy working in the field of visual arts. His ''people'' skills were considerably lower than his ''task'' skills.

A few months later, Bill returned to the career counselor. He said, ''For the first time in my life, I feel directed. I love my new job at Acme Studios. I accept my parents' interests and values, but more importantly, I have to be able to identify and accept my own. I no longer try to please my parents first.''

COMMENTS:

CASE 3

WHEN ONE FEELS SUPPORTED AND ENCOURAGED BY OTHERS

Frank is a 43-year-old engineer, married for twenty years with three teenage children. He has worked for the same company since graduating from college. He admitted that he did not believe in seeking help but was so discouraged and in such pain, he did not know what else to do. Frank, on the recommendation of a friend, made an appointment with a psychologist. Frank said:

''I know that I want to leave my present company but do not know where to go or what to do.''

After four sessions of counseling, Frank made the following comments: ''I am finding the counseling sessions most helpful. I felt great fear of the unknown initially, but you have helped me realize my situation is not all that unique and that my skills are competitive. Thanks to your encouragement, I am anxious to quietly start searching for a new position.''

COMMENTS:

CASE 4

> ## WHEN ONE SEES SUCCESS FROM REALIZING A GOAL

Jane is a 35-year-old single woman employed in the human resources field. She was unhappy with her job, and increasingly anxious about not being married. Jane met with a friend who was also in the human resources field and confided:

"Until recently, I never really believed in the importance of writing down my goals. It all seemed so silly to me until you told me how you were able to accomplish things if you wrote out specific goals. Thanks to you, I have completed two self-improvement projects at work. I have also lost five pounds because of a new goal to exercise four days each week. My energy is now focused on what I want. Things are looking up."

COMMENTS:

CASE 5

WHEN ONE BETTER UNDERSTANDS WHO THEY ARE AND CAN APPRECIATE THEIR STRENGTHS

Tom, a 55-year-old executive, has been outplaced after working for the same company thirty years. He was feeling very confused, depressed and lost. During his first visit to an outplacement counselor, he said:

''I just don't understand. How could they do that after all the years I have given. Isn't my loyalty important? It just is not fair. My wife is more upset than I am. The company has been her family as well as mine.''

After working with Tom for two months, the counselor was able to help Tom turn his thinking around.

Last week Tom said:

''Taking time to really stop and evaluate myself, to examine my strengths, weaknesses, likes, dislikes and goals has helped me be psychologically prepared for a job search and has strengthened my relationship with my wife.''

COMMENTS:

WHAT OTHERS HAVE DONE TO INCREASE THEIR FEELINGS OF SELF-ESTEEM?

The following comments have been offered by participants from self-esteem workshops about specific things that have helped them develop better self-esteem.

My self-esteem improved because:

- I solicited feedback from peers.

- I practiced positive thinking and visualized success.

- I sought counseling to help me through difficult times.

- I identified my values and then made them priorities.

- I improved my ability to meet new challenges and risk changes.

- I read a lot of positive literature.

- I regularly attended support groups.

- I learned to be honest in expressing my strengths, talents and skills.

- I wrote down my accomplishments on a daily basis.

- I found a new job and experienced success in that job.

- I discovered that my parents and friends believed in me.

- I made myself do things without waiting for others to suggest action.

- I took action on ideas I believed in.

- I made a definite effort to improve my personal appearance.

- I enrolled in a "Toastmasters" class to overcome my fear of public speaking.

- I took a battery of tests to identify my strengths.

- I went back to school.

- I practiced meditation and exercised daily.

> ### *The Dilemma*
> #### Author Unknown
>
> *''To laugh is to risk appearing a fool.*
> *To weep is to risk appearing sentimental.*
> *To reach out for another is to risk involvement.*
> *To expose feelings is to risk rejection.*
> *To place your dreams before the crowd is to risk ridicule.*
> *To love is to risk not being loved in return.*
> *To go forward in the face of overwhelming odds is to risk failure.*
>
> *But risks must be taken because the greatest hazard in life is to risk nothing. The person who risks nothing does nothing, has nothing, is nothing. He may avoid suffering and sorrow, but he cannot learn, feel, change, grow or love. Only a person who risks is free.''*

OVERCOMING FEAR

INSTRUCTIONS:

1. Write down the greatest fear that you have overcome.

2. Write a brief statement about how you overcame your fear. What did you do, how did you do it and what feelings did you have afterward?

FOUR STEPS TO OVERCOME FEAR

"Your belief at the beginning of a doubtful undertaking is the one thing that insures the successful outcome of your venture."

William James

1. Identify what exactly you fear most.
Example. My greatest fear is getting up in front of a large group to give a speech.

2. Write down everything you think could go wrong if you did what you are most fearful of.
Example. What could go wrong if I gave a speech?

    —I could forget what I was going to say.
    —People might laugh at me for sounding so dumb or silly.
    —I could tremble or even faint.

3. Take your greatest fear and develop a plan, step by step, outlining specific ways to overcome your fear.
Example. What can I do to overcome my fear of public speaking?

    —I could join Toastmasters or a similar group.
    —I could seek out activities where I could observe speakers in action (school, at work, seminars, church, etc.) and ask them how they do it.
    —I could take a public speaking class at a community college.
    —I could read a self-improvement book such as *Effective Presentation Skills*.*
    —I could try my hand at a simple public speaking effort like asking a question in a group session.

4. VERBALIZE your feelings of fear out loud.
    VISUALIZE yourself doing what you fear.
      PRACTICE thoroughly what you have prepared.
        EXPERIENCE the total process by breaking your fear into manageable parts.

---

*For an excellent book, order *Effective Presentation Skills* by Steve Mandell using the information in the back of this book.

EXPECT THE BEST AND GET IT RIGHT! PRACTICE MAKES PERFECT.

Take the FOUR STEPS TO OVERCOME FEAR outlined on the previous page and put them to work.

Case: Your boss has asked you to give a talk to a group of managers about a new accounting system. She assures you that you will do a good job and tells you that you have *three weeks* to prepare. Panic strikes! You have never had to do this before. Your first step is to outline and then write out exactly what you need to say.

HOW TO OVERCOME FEAR

First Week

- Stand in front of a mirror with the door closed. Stand erect, stomach in, chest out, head up, shoulders back and breathe deeply three to four times until you feel relaxed.

- Look yourself in the eye and repeat your fear aloud. Tell yourself the following: ''With practice I am going to give a very good talk.'' Smile!

- Carry on a series of conversations with yourself. Make certain that you look yourself in the EYE and keep a SMILE on your face.

- Practice reading your paper aloud. If possible, use a tape recorder to record your voice and play it back to hear the tone of your voice. Make certain you work on sounding enthusiastic because enthusiasm is contagious.

- Once you begin to feel comfortable, continue practicing your talk aloud, but concentrate on your posture and facial expressions as you look in the mirror.

- Practice twice a day if possible.

FOUR STEPS TO OVERCOME FEAR (continued)

Second Week

- Now it is time to give your speech to family members or friends. Invite them to sit in your living room, and pretend you have an audience. Concentrate on your voice and the content of your talk.

    * Continue to practice several times during the week. Use a mirror as often as you can.

Third Week   Time is drawing close!

- It is time to practice twice a day, once in front of the mirror and another time to yourself. Practice on the way to work, before going to bed, during your coffee break or during lunch—anytime you have an opportunity. As you practice:

    * IMAGINE/VISUALIZE/PICTURE yourself speaking in a room surrounded by friends and peers.

    * IMAGINE being in the audience observing YOURSELF doing an excellent job as the speaker.

The Day of the Speech

- Arrive early to double-check the room.

- Keep your notes handy in a readable, organized fashion.

- Practice walking to the front of the room.

- Ask a friend to listen to your "dry run" to make sure your voice is appropriate for the size of the room.

- Relax, and tell yourself no one has ever been better prepared.

- Do a great job!

SUMMARY

Practice makes perfect and practice reduces fear.

Overcoming fear of any kind, including asking for a raise, leaving a relationship, learning to drive a car, assuming a new position or changing careers, takes time. By breaking down your fears into manageable parts, your anxieties can be overcome in time. The need to verbalize, visualize, practice and experience that which you are most fearful about is crucial. Also, knowing what it is that you need to do (i.e., having a solution) gives you a sense of control and allows you to redirect your thinking and energy.

OVERCOME FEAR BY:

• Assessing what it is that makes you most afraid.

• Writing a script of action that needs to be taken. Role-play the action steps with a friend.

• Asking for advice. Gather information and seek help.

• Involving yourself with activities directly related to your fears.

• Seeking and associating with others involved in similar activities. Develop a positive support system.

• Creating a NOW attitude. Act on positive ideas, thoughts and impulses. Do not wait until you think you are an expert.

• If you do not succeed the first time, try again.

VERBALIZE, VISUALIZE, PRACTICE and EXPERIENCE YOUR FEAR
UNTIL IT NO LONGER DOMINATES YOUR LIFE.

SECTION THREE

CREATE A POSITIVE BELIEF SYSTEM

"No one can make you feel inferior without your consent."

Eleanor Roosevelt

"Whatever the mind can conceive and believe, it can achieve."

Napoleon Hill

Many people feel that the number one roadblock to success is the inability to believe in oneself. We often tend to overlook our strengths and focus on our limitations. We concentrate on self-defeating negative attitudes formulated in our early years. When we can turn those negative thoughts around and focus on our strengths, we will enjoy a positive belief system. A positive belief system encourages an optimistic, positive attitude. I have heard it said that one's attitude toward oneself is the single most important factor in healing or staying well. Such a belief system allows you to think and act in a positive way. This, in turn, leads to positive results both at work and at home.

It has been said that success is 80 percent attitude and 20 percent aptitude. In other words, our natural talents are not as important as what we do with them.

CREATE A POSITIVE BELIEF SYSTEM AT WORK

> "When you expect the best, your mind focuses on the best."

When you get up in the morning, you have two choices.

> 1. "Today is going to be a wonderful day."
>
> or
>
> 2. "Today is going to be a lousy day."

The choice is yours. What will you choose? Your outlook has a definite affect on how you will feel. Your choice of words can change your thoughts. These thoughts can change your life.

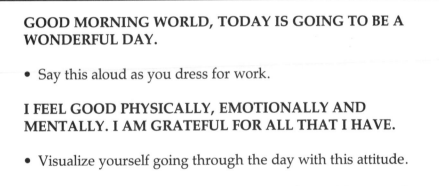

GOOD MORNING WORLD, TODAY IS GOING TO BE A WONDERFUL DAY.

- Say this aloud as you dress for work.

I FEEL GOOD PHYSICALLY, EMOTIONALLY AND MENTALLY. I AM GRATEFUL FOR ALL THAT I HAVE.

- Visualize yourself going through the day with this attitude.

- Greet your co-workers with a **SMILE** and a positive remark. Look them in the eye as you begin each day.

As the day progresses, you may find your positive attitude beginning to waver. Someone has pushed your wrong button. Feelings of anger, stress, self-doubt begin to creep into your mind. Now what?

> **I CAN'T; I DON'T WANT TO; I AM FEELING STRESSED.**

Research suggests that as much as 80 percent of all disease may originate from stress. People bring their personal problems to work and their work problems home. Absenteeism, tardiness and low performance is directly related to stress.

CREATE A POSITIVE BELIEF SYSTEM AT WORK (continued)

> Simple 30-second suggestions for turning your stress into positive energy

Stress reduction strategies are well known. Yoga, physical exercise, meditation, visual imagery and biofeedback are a few examples. Each person deals with stress a little differently.

Try any of these temporary suggestions to see what happens to your energy level when you start to feel uptight.

You have 30 seconds for each idea.

STRESS REDUCERS

Close your eyes and picture the most beautiful sunset you have ever seen.

What was your favorite movie and why?

How many state capitals can you think of—say out loud.

Draw as many flying objects as you can think of.

You have just won one million dollars. What are the first five things you plan on doing?

Say out loud all the names you can think of that begin with the letter ''J.''

What do these mean to you?

$$\frac{\text{stand}}{\text{I}}$$

(I understand)

$$|R|E|A|D|I|N|G|$$

(reading between the lines)

LEARN TO TURN NEGATIVE THINKING PATTERNS AROUND

- Sit quietly at your desk for a few minutes the next time you feel depressed or angry and let your mind wander.

    When you are relaxed, ask yourself, ''Why am I so angry?'' ''What is really going on?''

    Mentally review what is frustrating you. Try to identify whether it is fear, insecurity, regret or guilt.

    Then share those frustrations with a friend instead of holding them inside. Address your needs but also be willing to listen to the needs and responses of others.

- Keep a journal of your negative feelings and analyze what you have written to learn why you feel the way you do.

MY FRUSTRATION JOURNAL

Feelings	When	What occurred	Reaction

LEARN TO TURN NEGATIVE THINKING PATTERNS AROUND (continued)

- When you hear others speak in negative terms, try interjecting new ideas, optimistic thoughts or satisfying expressions. Then listen to their response. Often you will be able to change the focus from negative to positive.

- Be direct with individuals who constantly complain or give negative messages.

  "I am working on creating a more positive attitude for myself and would appreciate your support," or "No matter what you may say or think about me, I am a capable person."

- Use Self-Talk/Self-Imaging

  —Think in terms of "can" when you hear yourself saying, "I can't."

  —Imagine: You are about to engage in an important interview. You think to yourself, "I am not going to get this job," "I am not qualified."

  —At this point you need to STOP and think: "I'll give it my best effort." "I can do it." "I have what it takes!"

  —Before leaving for the interview, look at yourself in the mirror and repeat again, "I have what it takes."

- One of my favorite sayings is "Success comes in cans and failure comes in can'ts."

- When all else fails, take a quiet moment, look out the window, take a walk, pick up a magazine that holds your interest. Do anything to divert your attention from your negative feelings. Learn to let go and move on from unhappy memories. Freeing yourself from resentments creates new positive energy.

LEARN TO IMPROVE YOUR INTERPERSONAL COMMUNICATION

Not everyone has an outgoing personality or is verbally adept. It is possible, however, to improve your interpersonal communication abilities through practice. Some suggestions include:

- Analyze the quality of your conversations with others.

  —If your conversations revolve exclusively around you, become an active listener and engage others in conversation.

  —When in doubt about what to say, **ASK THE QUESTIONS, WHAT, WHERE, WHEN, WHY and HOW.** Everyone loves to be asked an opinion and to talk about themselves.

  —Think of new topics. Read stimulating articles. Keep up with current events or develop a new hobby.

- Make a mental picture of the ideal you. Hold that image in your mind before you speak and begin acting accordingly.

- Lend a helping hand to others. Remember how happy you feel when giving a gift to one in need, listening to one who is hurting or volunteering for needy cause. Love grows when you give it away.

- Finally, write a letter to those you would like to forgive. Read it out loud until you have let go.

"When you talk, your words, feelings and body must be in harmony. To achieve this harmony know how you really feel. Express these feelings through your words, tone of voice and body language."

Virginia Satir

LEARN TO EXPAND YOUR SUPPORT SYSTEM AT WORK

Create a positive environment for yourself. Surround yourself with positive people.

- Think about who you spend the majority of your time with on the job. Are they exerting a positive influence on your life? Ask yourself, "Who do I usually have lunch with? Is it the same people daily, weekly, monthly? Would I benefit by seeking some new relationships?"

List Your Support System/Network

Write the names of those you count on for support in the areas listed. Don't worry if you leave a blank; this is simply a way for you to "take a snapshot" of your present support group and to alert you to any gaps you may wish to fill.

Financial matters: _____

Legal matters: _____

Work-related matters: _____

Medical/dental: _____

Personal: _____

Social: _____

Religious: _____

Educational: _____

Others: _____

*Could you call on the people you listed for support?

*Are individuals in your support system aware of your abilities and aspirations?

*Are you aware of how your support system members can help you?

EXPAND YOUR PROFESSIONAL DEVELOPMENT

Normally the better prepared you are for your career, the higher your self-confidence and self-esteem. There are almost unlimited opportunities for ongoing self-improvement. Following are a few suggestions. Check those with which you agree. To improve my professional development, I will:

☐ Seek extra training or education. Attend seminars, conferences, lectures and workshops off the job. Check local college bulletins, business trade journals and newspapers for updated information about ways to continue expanding my knowledge.

☐ Once a month ask myself, ''Am I giving 100 percent to my job? Do I have a positive attitude about my work? Why did I take the job and how has it changed. How have I changed?''

☐ Update my **RÉSUMÉ** and continue doing so once every six months.

☐ Jot down in my daily calendar before leaving work each day, ''**WHAT I ACCOMPLISHED TODAY.**''

☐ Seek new challenges at work. Request a new assignment or an additional one. Ask, rather than waiting to be asked, for what I want.

☐ Pretend I am the boss and picture what my organization needs; then take steps to address those needs.

BALANCE YOUR LIFE!

> **INSTRUCTIONS:**
>
> Check any of the following that applies to you:

☐ 1. I always take work home at night.

☐ 2. Work pressures affect my relationships with family and friends.

☐ 3. I cannot turn off "work thoughts" once at home.

☐ 4. I find myself solving work-related problems in the middle of the night.

☐ 5. I use weekends to catch up on work-related projects.

☐ 6. I "check in" at work even during days off.

☐ 7. I market myself and my job during social gatherings.

☐ 8. Even personal conversations center around my work.

☐ 9. In many ways, my identity is my job.

☐ 10. I do not feel balance between my personal life and my work.

If you checked more than two of the above questions, you should re-evaluate your priorities in terms of BALANCE.*

> We cannot easily separate our career from our personal life. Balance is the key. Learning how to let go of work and take the time for family, self or friends is very important. Self-esteem is the bridge between who you are and what you do **both at work and at home**.

*For an excellent book, order *Balancing Home and Career* by Pam Conrad using the information in the back of this book.

BALANCE YOUR LIFE!
AT HOME

FIVE WAYS TO BUILD SELF-ESTEEM
FOR CHILDREN*

1. DEVELOP A SENSE OF SECURITY.

Children need well-defined limits. They need to know what is expected of them with **FIRMNESS, FAIRNESS, FRANKNESS and FONDNESS.**

2. DEVELOP A SELF-IDENTITY OR SELF-CONCEPT.

If a child sees him- or herself as having potential in a particular area, he or she will try to develop his or her skills in that area. Treat your child as if he or she belonged to your best friend. Teach your child about uniqueness and develop his or her interests.

3. DEVELOP A SENSE OF BELONGING.

Parents need to teach family tradition and be a support group. Give positive feedback and spend quality time.

4. DEVELOP A SENSE OF PURPOSE.

FOCUS the child's energy. Children need to know, WHO AM I? DO YOU LOVE ME AND CARE FOR ME? WHAT CAN I DO? Achievement comes about because of high expectations and a high level of support.

5. DEVELOP A SENSE OF POWER OR PERSONAL CONFIDENCE.

Encourage children to set goals for themselves, learn about their options and evaluate how they are doing.

---

*Reprinted with permission from *Building Self-Esteem: A Parent's Guide* by Robert Reasoner, Consulting Psychologist Press, Inc., Palo Alto, CA 94306

Developing Self-Esteem

10 KEYS TO DEVELOPING SELF-ESTEEM IN CHILDREN

If you have (or plan) children, the following advice is excellent. The National Institute of Mental Health asked 50 parents who had raised their children to become well-adjusted, productive adults the following question:

''Based on your personal experiences, what is the best advice you can give new parents about raising children?'' Following is a summary of their responses:

1. LOVE ABUNDANTLY. The most important task is to love and really care about your child. This gives him or her a sense of security, belonging and support. It smoothes out the rough edges of society.

2. DISCIPLINE CONSTRUCTIVELY. Give clear direction and enforce the limits on your child's behavior. Emphasize ''Do this,'' instead of ''Don't do that.''

3. WHENEVER POSSIBLE, SPEND TIME WITH YOUR CHILDREN. Play with them, talk to them, teach them to develop a family spirit and give them a sense of belonging.

4. GIVE THE NEEDS OF YOUR MATE PRIORITY. A husband and wife are more likely to be successful parents when they put their marriage first. Don't worry about the children getting ''second best.'' Child-centered households produce neither happy marriages nor happy children.

5. TEACH YOUR CHILDREN RIGHT FROM WRONG. They need to be taught basic values and manners so that they will get along well in society. Insist that they treat others with kindness, respect and honesty. Set personal examples of moral courage and integrity.

6. DEVELOP MUTUAL RESPECT. Act in a respectful way toward your children. Say ''please'' and ''thank you,'' and apologize when you are wrong. Children who are treated with respect will then know how to treat you and others respectfully.

7. LISTEN. REALLY LISTEN. This means giving your children undivided attention, putting aside your beliefs and feelings and trying to understand your children's point of view.

8. OFFER GUIDANCE. Be brief. Don't give speeches. And don't force your opinions on your children.

9. FOSTER INDEPENDENCE. Gradually allow children more freedom and control over their lives. One parent said, ''Once your children are old enough, phase yourself out of the picture, but always be near when they need you.''

10. BE REALISTIC, EXPECT TO MAKE MISTAKES. Be aware that outside influences such as peer pressure will increase as children mature. Don't expect things to go well all the time. Child-rearing has never been easy. It has its sorrows and heartaches, but it also has rewards and joys.

BALANCE YOUR LIFE!
AT HOME (continued)

MAKE TIME FOR YOU

All work and no play is not fun. When you are feeling rushed, rattled and full of self-doubt, step back and look for options. Let your creative powers take over. Only when you stop doing things that don't work can you develop a positive approach to your life. Following are some ideas. Check any you plan to try. I will:

☐ Make an appointment with myself, or skip lunch, or drive to work a new way.

☐ Interrupt my routine during the middle of the week and try a new eating place or buy a sandwich and sit outside.

☐ Start a regular exercise routine, take dance lessons, go bike riding or go for evening walks.

☐ Unplug my T.V. for one week. Spend my new time listening to my favorite music or reading a new book.

☐ Become a "tourist" in my own home town.

☐ Clean out my closet. If I have not worn something for a year, donate it to charity.

☐ Spend a leisurely hour soaking in the tub.

☐ Keep an ongoing IDEA notebook. Jot down my hunches and intuitions.

☐ Keep my mind alert and challenged by playing games and working puzzles.

☐ Start a discussion group, of others in my field, as a way of expanding my knowledge.

☐ Make a list of those whose company I most enjoy and plan a get-together.

☐ Visit my local book store and choose a new topic about which I know nothing.

☐ Become active in a cause in which I believe.

(Add others)

☐

☐

BELIEVE IN YOURSELF AND MAKE IT HAPPEN!

> **INSTRUCTIONS:** The following reminders can be posted on your mirror, refrigerator or desk or be given to friends who may need a little uplifting.

Things to Remember:

- Success is an attitude.

- Whatever your mind can conceive and believe, you can achieve.

- Dream great dreams and work to make them come true.

- You are unique and special.

- Never affirm self-limitations.

- To accomplish great things, you must believe, dream, plan and then act.

- Yes you can!

- Believing is magic.

- You can always better your previous best.

- You don't know what you can do until you try.

- There is no failure except in not trying.

- Defeat may test you; it need not stop you.

- If at first you don't succeed, try another approach.

- For every obstacle, there is a solution.

- Nothing in the world can take the place of persistence.

SUMMARY

"Self-Esteem means believing in yourself."

Too many people relate only to the negatives in life. By being observant, aware, and trying new approaches to self-defeating belief patterns, you will be able, in time, to turn those feelings around. Nothing happens overnight and what may work for one may not work for another.

NEVER, NEVER GIVE UP. By verbalizing and thinking in terms of the positives, your subconscious will affect your conscious mind, causing you to **ACT not react.**

It is true that the things we expect, believe and tell ourselves daily affect not only what we accomplish at work, but also how we feel and behave at home. Change takes time and perseverance. Stay at it and slowly you will see your self-concept grow as messages of limitations are replaced by those of achievements and strengths.

KEYS TO REMEMBER

1. WHAT CAN YOU CONTROL? . . . . YOU, not others.

2. WHAT CAN YOU DO NOW? . . . . THINK STRENGTHS and POSITIVES.

3. WHAT DO YOU WANT TO DO? . . . . FOCUS YOUR THINKING.

4. WHAT DO YOU NEED TO DO? . . . . PRIORITIZE and FOCUS YOUR ENERGY NOW.

"The way you act will eventually be determined by the way you think, feel and believe."
Doug Hooper

P A R T

II

HOW TO MAKE
WHAT YOU WANT TO HAPPEN
COME TRUE

THIS PART WILL ALLOW YOU TO:

—IDENTIFY YOUR MARKETABLE CAREER STRENGTHS

—TAKE THE TIME TO DREAM

—DECIDE WHAT YOU WANT, WHEN AND HOW!

—TAKE ACTION FOR YOUR SUCCESS

SECTION FOUR

IDENTIFY YOUR MARKETABLE CAREER STRENGTHS

Job security is no longer a given for those who work hard and are loyal. This is an age of acquisitions, mergers, down-sizing and ''golden handshakes.'' You alone must take responsibility for your career. Too many people spend their life looking for a perfect job, career or relationship and end up getting hurt or being disappointed.

Time and energy can also be wasted waiting for change to happen. This includes waiting for recognition, promotion or to be discovered by others you hope will make decisions and choices for you.

To win at life, you need to accept the responsibility of your unique strengths. You can then use this knowledge to achieve success.

If positive change is to take place in your life, you must first be able to answer the following questions:

- **WHAT IS MY EXPERIENCE?**
- **WHO AM I TODAY?**
- **WHERE AM I HEADED?**

If you are willing to objectively **ANALYZE, IDENTIFY, ACCEPT and ACT** on your **STRENGTHS** you will be able to offset any limitations and succeed. This section will help you learn how to do this.

MY STRENGTHS INCLUDE:

IDENTIFY YOUR MARKETABLE CAREER STRENGTHS

The next few pages contain several exercises designed to help you focus on YOUR MARKETABLE CAREER STRENGTHS. You will be asked to analyze and review:

ONCE YOU HAVE COMPLETED THESE EXERCISES, A SUMMARY OVERVIEW WILL BE PROVIDED THAT WILL HELP YOU INTEGRATE THE RESULTS IN ORDER TO FOCUS MORE EFFECTIVELY ON YOUR CAREER.

EXERCISE 1
YOUR PAST BELIEF SYSTEM

INSTRUCTIONS:

1. Draw a line illustrating your life from birth to the present. Place an ''x'' on the line where you see yourself today. Be creative. Let your mind wander back to your childhood. Each person's line will be different because no two lives are the same in terms of positives or negatives, or memories.

2. Write in significant PEOPLE and EVENTS approximately where they belong on your ''life line.''

3. On a separate sheet of paper, briefly answer the following questions:

   —What influence did the people or events you highlighted have on your life?

   —What lessons did you learn?

   —Which significant events brought fond memories?

   —Do you see reoccurring highs and lows? Do you know why?

   —Where did you place your ''x''? How far beyond the ''x'' does your line extend? Are you looking forward to new and exciting experiences? Are you a good goal setter?

EXERCISE 2
WHO ARE YOU?
YOUR PERSONALITY STRENGTHS

Take time to think about your positive, personal characteristics that make you WHO YOU ARE TODAY. Everyone has positive qualities, but often, we do not take the time to identify them.

INSTRUCTIONS:

Circle those words that best describe how you see yourself today: your personality, character, intellect and outlook on life. Be as objective and realistic as possible.

accepting	enterprising	persuasive
achieving	entertaining	poised
active	enthusiastic	precise
adventurous	expressive	productive
affectionate	fair-minded	professional
ambitious	friendly	quick
articulate	gentle	rational
assertive	genuine	realistic
attractive	good-natured	receptive
caring	graceful	reassuring
charismatic	helpful	responsive
charming	humorous	self-aware
cheerful	happy	self-confident
committed	imaginative	sensitive
compassionate	independent	serious
confident	insightful	sincere
congenial	intelligent	skillful
conscientious	intuitive	sociable
considerate	knowledgeable	spontaneous
cooperative	logical	steady
creative	likable	stimulating
dedicated	open-minded	strong
dependable	optimistic	sympathetic
determined	objective	talented
disciplined	organized	thoughtful
distinctive	orderly	tolerant
dynamic	original	trusting
efficient	outgoing	truthful
empathetic	patient	unique
encouraging	perceptive	unpretentious
energetic	persistent	vigorous
		warm

EXERCISE 3
YOUR INTERESTS

INSTRUCTIONS:

(1) List 20 THINGS you enjoy doing. These may include hobbies, amusement, social activities, sports, classes, etc.

1. _____
2. _____
3. _____
4. _____
5. _____
6. _____
7. _____
8. _____
9. _____
10. _____
11. _____
12. _____
13. _____
14. _____
15. _____
16. _____
17. _____
18. _____
19. _____
20. _____

(2) Ask yourself the following:

—How often do you do those activities?
—Are there significant patterns? For example are the activities enjoyed alone or with others?
—What skills do you use most often? Physical, analytical, creative or verbal?

EXERCISE 4
YOUR CAREER/JOB
AND PERSONAL VALUES

"Clarifying your values is the essential first step towards a richer, fuller, more productive life."

Carl Rogers

Every decision you make in life is a reflection of what is important to you. Values are based on your belief system and your attitudes. Values reflect who you are and why you do what you do. Your values change as you change. When you have a conflict of values, this will bring personal and/or career dissatisfaction.

INSTRUCTIONS:

On the following pages (55 and 56) check the importance of each value in terms of your ideal working situation and personal life. Rate each as:

☐ Always important. A value you would like to have in your life every day.

☐ Often. A strong value, but not as important as always.

☐ Sometimes. Important, but you would be willing to compromise.

☐ Seldom. Not very important.

☐ Never. Holds no value to you.

VALUES EXERCISE

VALUES CHART	Always	Often	Sometimes	Seldom	Never
Advancement—Be able to get ahead rapidly, gaining opportunities for growth and seniority from work well done.					
Adventure—Have work duties that involve frequent risk-taking.					
Aesthetics—Be involved in studying or appreciating the beauty of things, ideas, etc.					
Affiliation—Be recognized as a member of a particular organization.					
Artistic Creativity—Engage in creative work in any of several art forms.					
Challenging Problems—Engage continually with complex questions and demanding tasks, trouble-shooting and problem-solving as a core part of a job.					
Change and Variety—Have work responsibilities frequently changed in content and setting.					
Community—Live in a town or city where I can meet my neighbors and become active in local politics or service projects.					
Competition—Engage in activities that pit my abilities against others.					
Creative Expression—Be able to express in writing and in person my ideas concerning the job and how I might improve it; have opportunities for experimentation and innovation.					
Creativity (general)—Create new ideas, programs, organized structures or anything else not following format developed by others.					
Excitement—Experience a high degree of stimulation or frequent novelty and drama on the job.					
Exercise Competence—Demonstrate a high degree of proficiency in job skills and knowledge; show above-average effectiveness.					

VALUES CHART	Always	Often	Sometimes	Seldom	Never
Fast Pace—Work in circumstances where there is high-pace activity and work done rapidly.					
Friendships—Develop close personal relationships with people as a result of work activity.					
Help Others—Be involved in helping people directly, either individually or in small groups.					
Help Society—Do something to contribute to the betterment of the world.					
High Earnings Anticipated—Be able to purchase essentials and the luxuries of life I wish.					
Independence—Be able to determine nature of work without significant direction from others; not have to follow instructions or conform to regulations.					
Influence People—Be in a position to change attitudes or opinions of other people.					
Intellectual Status—Be regarded as very well-informed and a strong theorist, as one acknowledged "expert" in a given field.					
Job Tranquility—Avoid pressures and "the rat race" in job role and work setting.					
Knowledge—Engage myself in pursuit of knowledge, truth and understanding.					
Location—Find place to live (town, geographic area) conducive to my lifestyle, a desirable home base for my leisure, learning and work life.					
Make Decisions—Have the power to decide courses of action, policies, etc.—a judgment job.					

Continue to next page

Developing Self-Esteem

VALUES EXERCISE (continued)

VALUES CHART	Always	Often	Sometimes	Seldom	Never
Moral Fulfillment—Feel that my work is contributing to ideals I feel are very important.					
Physical Challenge—Have a job that requires bodily strength, speed, dexterity or agility.					
Power and Authority—Control the work activities or partially control destinies of others.					
Precision Work—Deal with tasks that have exact specifications, that require careful, accurate attention to detail.					
Profit, Gain—Have strong likelihood of accumulating large amounts of money or other material gain through ownership, profit-sharing, commissions, merit pay increases and the like.					
Public Contact—Have a lot of day-to-day contact with people.					
Recognition—Get positive feedback and public credit for work well done.					
Security—Be assured of keeping my job and a reasonable financial reward.					
Stability—Have a work routine and job duties that are largely predictable and not likely to change over a long period of time.					
Status—Impress or gain the respect of friends, family and community by the nature and/or level of responsibility of my work.					
Supervision—Have a job in which I am directly responsible for work done by others.					
Time Freedom—Have responsibilities I can work at according to my time schedule; no specific working hours required.					

VALUES CHART	Always	Often	Sometimes	Seldom	Never
Work Alone—Do projects by myself, without any amount of contact with others.					
Work on Frontiers of Knowledge—Work in research and development, generating information and new ideas in the academic, scientific or business communities.					
Work Under Pressure—Work in time-pressured circumstances, where there is little or no margin for error, or with demanding personal relationships.					
Work with Others—Have close working relations with group, work as a team toward common goals.					
OTHERS					
Affection—caring, intimacy, love					
Appearance—physical attraction					
Community—political, service projects					
Family—caring for those you love					
Health—physical well being					
Fun—leisure play					
Devotion—strong faith					
Friendship—close friends					
Personal Growth—optimize personal development					

"Adapted from Career Values Card Sort ©1977 Richard Knowdell. This instrument is available from Career Research and Testing, 2005 Hamilton Ave., Suite 250, San Jose, Ca. 95125"

VALUES EXERCISE—SUMMARY

What are your career/job and personal values?

Review those items you checked "Always important" and select the top NINE.
(List them below. Include both career and personal values).

MY TOP VALUES ARE:

1 _____ : _____

2 _____ : _____

3 _____ : _____

4 _____ : _____

5 _____ : _____

6 _____ : _____

7 _____ : _____

8 _____ : _____

9 _____ : _____

Circle those values that are presently being met in your life.

SUMMARY OF EXERCISE

One job/career may not meet all of your values. It is important to look closely at your present position and see if you could change your job to include other important values. Assess your free-time activities also because one job may never meet all your values. BALANCE IS THE KEY.

EXERCISE 5
YOUR PERFORMANCE
APPRAISAL INVENTORY

Name _____ Date _____

Job Title _____ Department _____

Organization _____

INSTRUCTIONS:

As objectively as possible, rate yourself on the degree of success with which you perform your present assigned duties. These concepts characterize your job description, as well as your interpersonal and technical skills and abilities.

Carefully evaluate yourself on a scale of 1 through 5 as explained below. Fill in the box to the left of each item.

SCALE

5 = Exceptional ability to understand and perform.

4 = Strong ability to understand and perform.

3 = Average ability to understand and to achieve results.

2 = Fair ability to understand but below average.

1 = Needs further development to understand and to apply techniques.

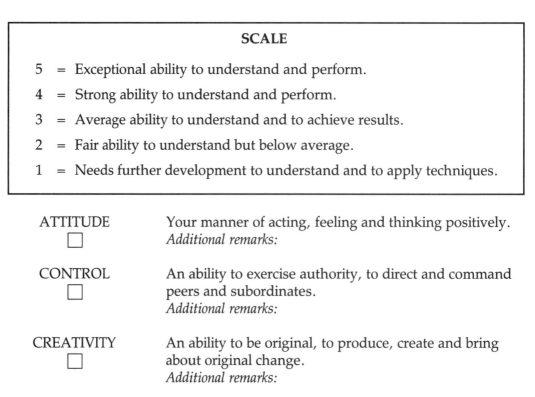

ATTITUDE
☐
Your manner of acting, feeling and thinking positively.
Additional remarks:

CONTROL
☐
An ability to exercise authority, to direct and command peers and subordinates.
Additional remarks:

CREATIVITY
☐
An ability to be original, to produce, create and bring about original change.
Additional remarks:

Continue to next page

DECISION MAKING ☐	An ability to define the problem, collect data and reach a conclusion. *Additional remarks:*
DELEGATION ☐	To entrust authority, responsibility and tasks to others. *Additional remarks:*
FLEXIBILITY ☐	An ability to adapt and change one's style to meet the needs of the situation and/or others. *Additional remarks:*
GROWTH POTENTIAL ☐	An ability to move vertically or horizontally in the corporate structure, to advance professionally. *Additional remarks:*
IMPACT ☐	An ability to produce changes in others. *Additional remarks:*
INDEPENDENCE ☐	Freedom of influence, control or determination of others. *Additional remarks:*
INITIATIVE ☐	An ability to originate new ideas or methods, to think or act without guidance from others. *Additional remarks:*
LEADERSHIP ☐	An ability to direct, command and guide others. *Additional remarks:*
LISTENING SKILLS ☐	An ability to be empathetic and supportive, to pick out important information and to give back to others. *Additional remarks:*
PLANNING ☐	An ability to devise, design and construct objectives to achieve goals. *Additional remarks:*
POLITICAL SKILLS ☐	An ability to function effectively within an organization with both staff and management. *Additional remarks:*

YOUR PERFORMANCE APPRAISAL INVENTORY (continued)

PRESENTATION
SKILLS
☐

An ability to speak in front of a small or large group of people.
Additional remarks:

QUALITY OF
WORK
☐

A desire to attain excellence in work produced.
Additional remarks:

RISK TAKING
☐

An ability to risk change and take chances.
Additional remarks:

SALES ABILITY
☐

An ability to convince, persuade and present information to others.
Additional remarks:

STRESS
☐

An ability to work under pressure or in strained situations.
Additional remarks:

TEAM BUILDING
☐

To join in cooperative activities with others for the unity and efficiency of a group.
Additional remarks:

TECHNICAL
COMPETENCE
☐

Being capable and qualified to perform in your given field.
Additional remarks:

VERBAL SKILLS
☐

An ability to express yourself verbally in group and individual situations.
Additional remarks:

VOLUME OF WORK
☐

An ability to be a top-producing employee who has a high level of productivity.
Additional remarks:

WRITTEN SKILLS
☐

To communicate an idea, report or letter in a clear and concise form.
Additional remarks:

YOUR PERFORMANCE APPRAISAL INVENTORY—SUMMARY

Place an "x" in the box where you see yourself today.

SCALE

☐   5 = Exceptional Performance: I believe I have mastered all elements of my present position.

☐   4 = Super Performance: I have a full understanding of my present position.

☐   3 = Good Performance: I understand the elements of my position and perform that which is expected.

☐   2 = Marginal Performance: I am not performing all elements of my job and would like guidance.

☐   1 = Areas Needing Further Development: I am very dissatisfied and further training, education, a transfer or change may be necessary.

Reprinted with permission from FOCUS: A Professional Development Program by C. Palladino, Consulting Psychologist Press, Inc., Palo Alto, CA 94306

For a complete review of the performance appraisal process, order *Effective Performance Appraisals* by Robert Maddux, using the information in the back of this book.

EXERCISE 6
YOUR JOB ASSESSMENT INVENTORY

For you, career satisfaction may mean money and financial security. For others it may mean recognition, greater achievement potential or redefining present job responsibilities.

INSTRUCTIONS:

Rate your present position in terms of your satisfaction:

	Low	Average	High
Kind of work	_____	_____	_____
Challenge in work	_____	_____	_____
Physical surroundings	_____	_____	_____
Co-workers' support	_____	_____	_____
Supervisor/management support	_____	_____	_____
Opportunity to make decisions	_____	_____	_____
Impact on the organization	_____	_____	_____
Company procedures/policies	_____	_____	_____
Job security	_____	_____	_____
Promotion/growth/opportunity	_____	_____	_____
Salary/vacations/benefits	_____	_____	_____
Work pressure	_____	_____	_____
Sense of achievement	_____	_____	_____
Recognition	_____	_____	_____

MOST IMPORTANT JOB DUTIES/RESPONSIBILITIES

(1) List your primary duties. Check the degree of challenge and enjoyment found in each.

Duty	Challenge			Enjoyment		
	Low	Average	High	Low	Average	High
1. _____	_____	_____	_____	_____	_____	_____
2. _____	_____	_____	_____	_____	_____	_____
3. _____	_____	_____	_____	_____	_____	_____
4. _____	_____	_____	_____	_____	_____	_____
5. _____	_____	_____	_____	_____	_____	_____

(2) List those duties you prefer not to do even though you are qualified.

_____   _____

_____   _____

_____   _____

_____   _____

(3) List those duties you would like to perform if you had a choice, training or education.

_____   _____

_____   _____

_____   _____

YOUR JOB ASSESSMENT INVENTORY (continued)

FUTURE PROJECTION

Check the importance of the following:

	Very Important	Somewhat Important	Not Important
Education:			
On-the-job training	————	————	————
Continuing formal education	————	————	————
Earning degrees: B.A., M.A., Ph.D.	————	————	————
Self-development programs	————	————	————

	Very Important	Somewhat Important	Not Important
Advancement:			
Opportunity for advancement and professional development	————	————	————
Opportunity to supervise	————	————	————
Advancement to high-level supervision	————	————	————
Advancement to top management	————	————	————

Reprinted with permission from FOCUS: A Professional Development Program by C. Palladino, Consulting Psychologist Press, Inc., Palo Alto, CA 94306

EXERCISE 7
YOUR SKILL STRENGTHS

Do you find yourself saying, "I am unmarketable. I have little going for me"?

Skills are the ability to perform a task in a competent manner, to be proficient in some activity. *The Dictionary of Occupational Titles* delineates three basic types of skills. The first, *Functional-Transferable* skills, are natural skills that show up early in your life. The second, *Self Management* skills, are considered personality traits. The third type, *Work-Content* skills, are the technical, specialized abilities you acquire through formalized education or training.

INSTRUCTIONS:

(1) Read through all the skills listed on pages 66 and 67 and CHECK those where you feel most HIGHLY PROFICIENT.

(2) Read back over the list and CHECK those skills that you would DELIGHT IN USING, ENJOY USING VERY MUCH or LIKE USING (one check for each skill).

(3) Then see the summary on pages 68–70 to determine if action is required on your part.

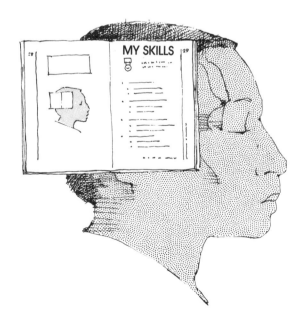

SKILL DESCRIPTIONS

SKILLS	HIGHLY PROFICIENT	TOTAL DELIGHT	ENJOY MUCH	LIKE	SKILLS	HIGHLY PROFICIENT	TOTAL DELIGHT	ENJOY MUCH	LIKE
Act as Liaison—Represent, serve as link between individuals or groups.					**Interview for Information**—Draw out subjects through incisive questioning.				
Analyze—Break down, figure out problems logically.					**Maintain Records**—Keep accurate and up-to-date records, log, record, itemize, collate, tabulate data.				
Budget—Economize, save, stretch money or other resources.					**Make Arrangements**—Coordinate events and handle logistics.				
Classify—Group, categorize, systematize data, people or things.					**Make Decisions**—Make major, complex or frequent decisions.				
Compose Music—Write and arrange music for voice or instruments.					**Mediate**—Manage conflict, reconcile differences.				
Counsel—Facilitate insight and personal growth, guide, advise, coach students, employees or clients.					**Monitor**—Keep track of the movement of data, people or things.				
Count—Tally, calculate, compute quantities.					**Motivate**—Recruit involvement, mobilize energy, stimulate peak performance.				
Deal with Feelings—Draw out, listen, accept, empathize, express sensitivity, defuse anger, calm, inject humor, appreciate.					**Negotiate**—Bargain for rights or advantages.				
Design—Structure new or innovative practices, programs, products, or environments.					**Observe**—Study, scrutinize, examine data, people or things scientifically.				
Entertain, Perform—Amuse, sing, dance, act, play music for, give a demonstration to, speak to an audience.					**Perceive intuitively**—Sense, show insight and foresight.				
Estimate—Appraise value or cost.					**Plan, Organize**—Define goals and objectives, schedule and develop projects or programs.				
Evaluate—Assess, review, critique feasibility or quality.					**Plant, Cultivate**—Grow food, flowers, trees or lawns—prepare soil, plant, water, fertilize, weed, harvest, trim, prune, mow.				
Expedite—Speed up production or services, trouble-shoot problems, streamline procedures.					**Portray Images**—Sketch, draw, illustrate, paint, photograph.				
Generate Ideas—Reflect upon, conceive of, dream up, brainstorm ideas.					**Prepare Food**—Wash, cut, blend, bake and arrange for nutrition, taste and aesthetics.				
Host/Hostess—Make welcome, put at ease, provide comfort and pleasure, serve visitors, guests or customers.					**Produce Skilled Crafts**—Shape, weave, attach, etch or carve ornamental gift or display items.				
Implement—Provide detailed follow-through of policies and plans.					**Proofread, Edit**—Check writings for proper usage and stylistic flair, make improvements.				
Initiate Change—Exert influence on changing the status quo, exercise leadership in bringing about new directions.									

SKILLS

Skill	HIGHLY PROFICIENT	TOTAL DELIGHT	ENJOY MUCH	LIKE
Read for Information—Research written resources efficiently and exhaustively.				
Sell—Promote a person, company, goods or services, convince of merits, raise money.				
Stage Shows—Produce theatrical, art, fashion or trade shows and other events for public performance or display.				
Supervise—Oversee, direct the work of others.				
Synthesize—Integrate ideas and information, combine diverse elements into a coherent whole.				
Teach, Train—Inform, explain, give instruction to students, employees or customers.				
Tend Animals—Feed, shelter, breed, train or show domestic pets, or farm or ranch animals.				
Test—Measure proficiency, quality, or validity, check and double-check.				
Transport—Drive, lift, carry or haul.				
Treat, Nurse—Heal, cure patients or clients.				
Use Carpentry Abilities—Construct, maintain or restore buildings, fittings or furnishings.				
Use Mechanical Abilities—Assemble, tune, repair or operate engines or other machinery.				
Use Physical Coordination and Agility—Walk, run, climb, scale, jump, balance, aim, throw, catch or hit.				
Visualize—Imagine possibilities, see in mind's eye.				
Write—Compose reports, letters, articles, ads, stories or educational materials.				

Adapted from *Motivated Skills Card Sort* ©1981 by Richard Knowdell. *This instrument is available from Career Research and Testing, 2005 Hamilton Ave., San Jose, Ca. 95125*

(1) List all of your "HIGHLY PROFICIENT" skills plus those skills that you checked under "TOTAL DELIGHT and ENJOY USING VERY MUCH"

1 _____
2 _____
3 _____
4 _____
5 _____
6 _____
7 _____
8 _____
9 _____
10 _____
11 _____
12 _____
13 _____
14 _____
15 _____
16 _____
17 _____
18 _____
19 _____
20 _____

(2) Circle duplicate skills that you identified as both Highly Proficient and Total Delight or Highly Proficient and Enjoy Using Very Much.

(3) Note the skills that you are using in your present job or would like to use. They are your skill strengths.

SKILL STRENGTH SUMMARY

Not all skills are learned at work or school. Transferable skills are learned during leisure activities as well as in a more formal professional setting.

INSTRUCTIONS:

1. Write ten comments describing your most satisfying experiences or achievements. An achievement is something you feel you have done well, either personally or professionally.

Examples of achievement:
- *Built a stereo set by myself from scratch.*
- *Published a short story my senior year of high school.*
- *Organized a successful surprise party for a friend.*
- *Persuaded management to accept my proposal.*

1 _____

2 _____

3 _____

4 _____

5 _____

6 _____

7 _____

8 _____

9 _____

10 _____

Continue to next page

2. Select five of your most positive experiences and briefly describe each. Use action verbs.

_____ *What were you doing?*
_____ *How did you do it?*
_____ *Where did you do it?*
_____ *Did your experience involve people, things, ideas?*
_____ *What did you enjoy most?*

1.

2.

3.

4.

5.

SKILL STRENGTH SUMMARY (continued)

3. Go back over each paragraph and look for repeated skill strength patterns that you used.

4. Circle the skill clusters BELOW that you found you used the **most**.

   A. MANUAL/MECHANICAL/OUTDOORS SKILLS: built, operated, constructed, moved, lifted, inspected, used mechanical or carpentry abilities.

   B. ANALYSIS/RESEARCH SKILLS: analyzed, researched, planned, invented, developed, tested, solved problems, collected, made decisions, assessed, gathered, interpreted, wrote.

   C. CREATIVE SKILLS: wrote, edited, published, decorated, designed, imagined, developed, visualized, conceptualized.

   D. VERBAL/MANAGEMENT/LEADERSHIP SKILLS: spoke, convinced, supervised, trained, developed ideas, led, persuaded, negotiated, lectured, debated, consulted, administered.

   E. HELP/SERVE/GUIDE/TEACH SKILLS: explained, listened, taught, encouraged, empathized, guided, helped, informed, cured, perceived, instructed, coached.

   F. DETAIL/NUMERICAL/FINANCIAL SKILLS: balanced, arranged, calculated, solved, collected, computed, counted, figured, audited, appraised, analyzed.

5. Compare this list with your skills chart. If there are similar patterns, this should be a good indication that you would be happy in a career that makes use of these skills.

6. Consider exploring new career opportunities based on your skill patterns. Your local college guidance center might be a good place to start.

EXERCISE 8
STYLES AND STRATEGIES
FOR SUCCESS

Review the statements below A, B, C, D. Then select the STYLE and STRATEGY that best describes how you perceive yourself. Keep in mind as you review your style and strategy that no one is totally one style. Most individuals do have a slight preference for one style over another.

A. COMPETENCE STYLE

Feelings of self-esteem may be enhanced when you feel competent and successful at what you have mastered. You may prefer projects and activities that are task oriented and where you can see an end result.

Low feelings of self-esteem may occur when you doubt your ability to master what you set out to do.

Strategies for Success

- Continue to update your skills by becoming an "expert" at what you are best at and enjoy.

- Reassess commitments, prioritize tasks and plan ahead for greater flexibility and long-term career planning.

- Record daily accomplishments and learn to accept and acknowledge personal praise and recognition when you have completed a task, project or activity.

B. SIGNIFICANCE STYLE

Feelings of self-esteem may be enhanced when you receive positive feedback from others and when you feel connected and are helping or caring for others.

Low feelings of self-esteem may occur when you feel harshly judged by others.

Strategies for Success

- Volunteer for a charitable organization or community service, or become active in or organize group projects and employee activities.

- Keep up with family and friends, entertain and start or join a support group.

STYLES AND STRATEGIES FOR SUCCESS SUMMARY (continued)

C. POWER STYLE

Feelings of self-esteem may increase when you feel you are influencing, controlling, persuading or inspiring others. Competition is challenged and satisfaction attained by accomplishing goals.

Low feelings of self-esteem may occur when you feel you have lost control.

Strategies for Success

- Become active in local or national politics.
- Participate in professional organizations and contribute by speaking, holding an office, writing or teaching on matters of importance to you.
- Set daily, weekly and yearly goals for yourself.

D. VIRTUE STYLE

Feelings of self-esteem may increase when you feel worthy, respected and competent. You value doing the right thing based on your strong beliefs.

Low feelings of self-esteem may occur when you feel diminished by criticism and feeling controlled or held to a tight schedule for any length of time.

Strategies for Success

- Find working environments that reflect your beliefs.
- Become active in community causes and issues that support your belief system.
- Help someone in need, support family traditions.
- Take up writing poetry and reading philosophy.

The key to enhanced self-esteem is to identify your self-esteem style and strategy and then try to create an environment that best supports your style. Becoming more aware and sensitive to the different styles of your family, friends and working colleagues will also add a new appreciation to their self-esteem strengths and differences.*

---

* Research on this model is presently being done by C. Palladino & Lynn Silton.

VERIFYING YOUR MARKETABLE CAREER STRENGTHS

The following exercises are designed to help you verify the marketable career strengths you identified beginning on page 49. The exercise forms in this section should be given to THREE SIGNIFICANT PEOPLE in your life whose opinions you value. Put your name and address at the top of each form so they can return them to you once they have finished filling them out.

The forms include:

- A PERFORMANCE APPRAISAL INVENTORY

- A PERSONALITY STRENGTHS SUMMARY

- A GENERAL ASSESSMENT REVIEW

We often become our own worst enemy. Receiving feedback from others whose opinions we value can be a very positive experience.

Asking others to evaluate your strengths may feel uncomfortable because it is not something we normally do. But the insight and knowledge you gain from others often helps you to enhance your feelings of self-esteem.

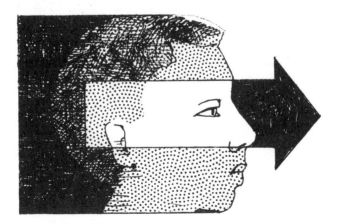

PERMISSION IS GRANTED BY THE PUBLISHER TO PHOTOCOPY THE FORMS ON PAGES 74–79.

PERFORMANCE APPRAISAL INVENTORY

Name _____ Date _____

Job Title _____ Department _____

Company _____

> As objectively as possible, please rate me on the degree of success with which you believe I perform my job. These concepts characterize my management, interpersonal and technical skills and abilities.

INSTRUCTIONS:

(1)   Carefully evaluate me on a scale of 1 through 5 as explained below. Fill in the box to the left of each item.

SCALE

5 = Exceptional Ability to understand and perform.

4 = Strong Ability to understand and perform.

3 = Average Ability to understand and to achieve results.

2 = Fair Ability to understand but below average.

1 = Needs Further Development to understand and to apply techniques.

ATTITUDE
☐

Your manner of acting, feeling and thinking positively.
Additional remarks:

CONTROL
☐

An ability to exercise authority, to direct and command peers and subordinates.
Additional remarks:

CREATIVITY
☐

An ability to be original, to produce, create and bring about original change.
Additional remarks:

Continue to next page

DECISION MAKING ☐	An ability to define the problem, collect data and reach a conclusion. *Additional remarks:*
DELEGATION ☐	To entrust authority, responsibility and tasks to others. *Additional remarks:*
FLEXIBILITY ☐	An ability to adapt and change your style to meet the needs of the situation and/or others. *Additional remarks:*
GROWTH POTENTIAL ☐	An ability to move vertically or horizontally in the corporate structure, to advance professionally. *Additional remarks:*
IMPACT ☐	An ability to produce changes in others. *Additional remarks:*
INDEPENDENCE ☐	Freedom of influence, control or determination of others. *Additional remarks:*
INITIATIVE ☐	An ability to originate new ideas or methods, to think or act without guidance from others. *Additional remarks:*
LEADERSHIP ☐	An ability to direct, command and guide others. *Additional remarks:*
LISTENING SKILLS ☐	An ability to be empathetic and supportive, to pick out important information and to give back to others. *Additional remarks:*
PLANNING ☐	An ability to devise, design and construct objectives to achieve goals. *Additional remarks:*
POLITICAL SKILLS ☐	An ability to function effectively within an organization with both staff and management. *Additional remarks:*

PERFORMANCE APPRAISAL INVENTORY
(continued)

PRESENTATION
SKILLS
☐

An ability to speak in front of a small or large group of people.
Additional remarks:

QUALITY OF
WORK
☐

A desire to attain excellence in work produced.
Additional remarks:

RISK TAKING
☐

An ability to risk change and take chances.
Additional remarks:

SALES ABILITY
☐

An ability to convince, persuade and present information to others.
Additional remarks:

STRESS
☐

An ability to work under pressure or in strained situations.
Additional remarks:

TEAM BUILDING
☐

To join in cooperative activities with others for the unity and efficiency of a group.
Additional remarks:

TECHNICAL
COMPETENCE
☐

Being capable and qualified to perform in your given field.
Additional remarks:

VERBAL SKILLS
☐

An ability to express yourself verbally in group and individual situations.
Additional remarks:

VOLUME OF WORK
☐

An ability to be a top-producing employee who has a high level of productivity.
Additional remarks:

WRITTEN SKILLS
☐

To communicate an idea, report or letter in a clear and concise form.
Additional remarks:

Place an "x" in the box where you see me today.

SCALE

☐ 5 = Exceptional Performance: You feel I have mastered all elements of my present position.

☐ 4 = Super Performance: You feel I have a full understanding of my present position.

☐ 3 = Good Performance: You believe I understand the elements of my position and perform that which is expected.

☐ 2 = Marginal Performance: You feel I am not performing all elements of my job and would like guidance.

☐ 1 = Areas Needing Further Development: You perceive I am dissatisfied and need further training, education or a transfer.

Return to address shown below when finished: Thank You.

[PRINT YOUR ADDRESS]

PERSONALITY STRENGTHS

Name: _____ Date _____

INSTRUCTIONS:

PLEASE CIRCLE THOSE WORDS THAT *YOU* BELIEVE *I* POSSESS. THINK OF THESE WORDS IN TERMS OF MY PERSONALITY, CHARACTER, INTELLECT AND OUTLOOK ON LIFE AS YOU KNOW ME. (Be objective and as realistic as possible.)

accepting	enterprising	persuasive
achieving	entertaining	poised
active	enthusiastic	precise
adventurous	expressive	productive
affectionate	fair-minded	professional
ambitious	friendly	quick
articulate	gentle	rational
assertive	genuine	realistic
attractive	good-natured	receptive
caring	graceful	reassuring
charismatic	helpful	responsive
charming	humorous	self-aware
cheerful	happy	self-confident
committed	imaginative	sensitive
compassionate	independent	serious
confident	insightful	sincere
congenial	intelligent	skillful
conscientious	intuitive	sociable
considerate	knowledgeable	spontaneous
cooperative	logical	steady
creative	likable	stimulating
dedicated	open-minded	strong
dependable	optimistic	sympathetic
determined	objective	talented
disciplined	organized	thoughtful
distinctive	orderly	tolerant
dynamic	original	trusting
efficient	outgoing	truthful
empathetic	patient	unique
encouraging	perceptive	unpretentious
energetic	persistent	vigorous
		warm

Return to address shown below when finished: Thank you.

[PRINT YOUR ADDRESS]

GENERAL ASSESSMENT REVIEW

Name: _____   Date _____

┌─────────────────────┐
│ **INSTRUCTIONS:** │
└─────────────────────┘

Please answer the following questions, as honestly as you can, as they apply to how you see me both personally and professionally.

1. What do you consider my greatest abilities?

    _____

    _____

2. What do you most admire about me?

    _____

    _____

3. What areas do you believe I need to develop further?

    _____

    _____

Describe briefly (one sentence or less) how you see me:

Emotionally _____

_____

Socially _____

_____

Intellectually _____

_____

Return to me at the following address when you are finished. Thank you.

[PRINT YOUR ADDRESS HERE]

MARKET YOURSELF FOR SUCCESS!

Once the evaluations have been returned, you are ready to summarize what you have learned about yourself. Spend an hour reviewing the exercises and thinking about how to integrate the results.

> **INSTRUCTIONS:** Write a letter describing the person reflected in the evaluations you received. Mention your strengths!

DATE:

DEAR SOMEBODY:

_____

_____

_____

_____

_____

_____

_____

_____

_____

_____

_____

                                        SINCERELY,

SUMMARY

The exercises in Section Four were designed to help you become more self-aware and inner-directed. The knowledge and information you gained as a result of these exercises should assist you in making conscious choices about what you want. They also encourage you to become an active partner in the process, instead of waiting for change to happen.

Professional and personal success can be yours, once you have studied, analyzed and identified your overall strength patterns.

Who you are today, an understanding of your personality traits, job performance, level of work satisfaction, interests, values and skills can be accepted, once they are identified. When this is achieved, a sense of wholeness and focus is possible and you can move ahead with a sense of confidence and energy.

This in turn can play a major role in feelings of high self-esteem, which leads to feeling unique, competent, secure, empowered and supportive of those with whom you come in contact.

"THINK YOU CAN, THINK YOU CAN'T, EITHER WAY YOU WILL BE RIGHT."

Henry Ford

SECTION FIVE

TAKE THE TIME TO DREAM!

> *"My painting has already taken form in my mind before I start on it. My first attempts are absolutely unbearable. I say this because I want you to know that if you see something worthwhile in what I am doing, it is not by accident, but because of real direction and purpose."*
>
> Vincent van Gogh

Does life seem to pass you by? Do you put your life in the hands of fate, other people, events, circumstances or even the stars? Or do you take charge and decide how, where, when, with whom and what type of life you want to live?

Once you are able to consciously take control of your thoughts, you can concentrate on your unique strengths and begin to realistically DREAM about what you want to do, have and be. Choice, not chance, will improve the quality of your life.

LEARN HOW TO "DREAM" FOR SUCCESS!

The ability to dream about what you want to do TODAY, TOMORROW or even FIVE YEARS from now is an important step in achieving self-esteem and success. Too few people take time to get in touch with their dreams or even stop long enough to think about WHAT THEY ARE or WHAT THEY WANT.

INSTRUCTIONS:

1. MAKE A LIST OF 15 OF YOUR WANTS, DREAMS and/or FANTASIES. Be as specific as you can. Can you see it, feel it, touch it, hear it, taste it and smell it?

2. Also MAKE A LIST OF 15 OF YOUR NEEDS.

WANTS	NEEDS
1.	1.
2.	2.
3.	3.
4.	4.
5.	5.
6.	6.
7.	7.
8.	8.
9.	9.
10.	10.
11.	11.
12.	12.
13.	13.
14.	14.
15.	15.

---

3. SELECT FIVE OF YOUR WANTS AND CREATE A REMINDER YOU CAN KEEP WITH YOU DAILY.

For example, you may have written "I want to own a Mercedes Benz." If so, buy a Mercedes key chain or put a picture of your dream car on the refrigerator to remind yourself of your dream.

KEEP A DAILY JOURNAL

INSTRUCTIONS:

1. Write down your feelings, experiences, emotions, daydreams, inspirations and desires. Keep the list going for one month. Let your mind describe anything at all about your life.

2. At the end of one month, carefully review what you have written. Summarize any direction (or lack of direction) that you notice. Be especially alert for any life dreams and make a separate list of them.

DREAM, DREAM, DREAM
WHERE DO YOU WANT TO BE
IN YOUR JOB/CAREER?

INSTRUCTIONS: Dream about your working day. Complete the following exercises as a way to focus your thoughts.

---

1. PLACE A PAD OF PAPER NEXT TO YOUR BED. EVERY MORNING WHEN YOU ARISE, JOT DOWN WHAT YOU WOULD LIKE TO DO IF YOU HAD TOTAL FREEDOM TO DECIDE HOW TO SPEND THAT DAY.

   Place each day's paper in an envelope after writing it. At the end of a month, reread them to see if there are patterns that you dream about.

2. A. WHAT WOULD BE YOUR IDEAL CAREER IF TRAINING OR FINANCES WERE NOT AN ISSUE?

   (1) _____

   (2) _____

   B. WHAT ASPECTS OF THIS IDEAL CAREER WOULD YOU FIND MOST SATISFYING?

   C. WHAT ARE THE LIMITATIONS OR ROADBLOCKS PREVENTING YOU FROM PURSUING THIS IDEAL CAREER/JOB?

YOUR CURRENT SELF-DESCRIPTION

INSTRUCTIONS:

A. DESCRIBE A TYPICAL DAY IN YOUR LIFE.

B. DIAGRAM A TYPICAL WEEK. (Use a circle, like the one shown below, that equals 168 hours). Note items such as work, sleep, home duties, sports, classes and social activities.)

TYPICAL WEEK (EXAMPLE)   YOUR TYPICAL WEEK

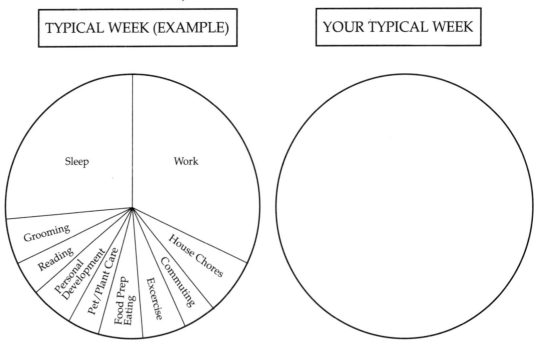

PROJECTED SELF-DESCRIPTION: FIVE YEARS FROM NOW

Take time to visualize what you want. Learn to feel it, hear it and see it every day.

INSTRUCTIONS:

A. DESCRIBE A TYPICAL DAY IN YOUR LIFE FIVE YEARS FROM NOW.

B. DIAGRAM YOUR IDEAL TYPICAL WEEK FIVE YEARS FROM NOW. (Use a circle similar to the one on page 86).

C. HOW IS THE "TODAY YOU" SIMILAR TO AND DIFFERENT FROM THE "YOU FIVE YEARS FROM NOW"? DESCRIBE THE DIFFERENCES AND HOW YOU FEEL ABOUT THEM.

SUMMARY

"If you can dream it and see it, you can achieve it."

The exercises in this section were designed to encourage you to reflect on the past and to spend time thinking about what is important, both personally and in your working life. Listing your wants and needs should help you focus on your dreams and the reality of having these dreams come true.

By projecting and thinking about your life in the future, you may have been able to gain insight into what you must do to begin making change happen. Once you decide you control what happens in your life, your self-esteem will be higher than with someone who simply takes life as it comes.

FROM DREAMS TO REALITY

SECTION SIX

DECIDE WHAT YOU WANT, WHEN AND HOW!

DECISIONS, DECISIONS, DECISIONS

Invest a few minutes each day to study, think and plan for tomorrow. This will help you achieve your dreams and improve your ability to make decisions that are based on a thought-out plan.

INSTRUCTIONS:

List any major decisions you are trying to make in your life. (Be as specific as possible; e. g., Do I want to go into sales? *not* Do I want to change jobs?)

1. _____

2. _____

3. _____

4. _____

5. _____

PERSONAL DECISION MAKING

Decision making can be an easy process if you remember to keep focused on what it is you are trying to decide.

FIVE STEPS TO BETTER DECISIONS

1. STATE YOUR DECISION IN WRITING.
   What decision are you trying to make? Describe in written form.

2. COLLECT DATA AND GATHER INFORMATION ON EACH DECISION.
   Be selective and put a time limit on your gathering of information.

3. MAKE A CHOICE.
   After information has been acquired and you have assessed the pros and cons of your decision, make a choice.

4. EXPERIENCE THE OUTCOME.
   Follow through. Let go of the ''what if'' thoughts and doubts. Focus your energy with a positive attitude and commitment.

5. EVALUATE THE OUTCOME.
   After a period of time, revisit the pros and cons of your decision. The worst outcome would be that it was the wrong decision. The good news is that you can define your new decision based on what you learned from your previous decision-making experience.

Decision making and goal setting go hand-in-hand. Once you are clear about how to make a decision, it is time to clarify the dreams you identified in SECTION FIVE and begin building a plan of action based on a sound decision-making process.

HOW TO PLAN FOR SUCCESS

People spend more time planning for a vacation than they do planning for what they want in life. To effectively plan for success, you must be clear about your long-range goals, map a route to reach them, set short-term goals and schedule time to pursue them. The nature of your goals is unimportant; what matters most is that you are able to define them and use them as a basis for planning.

1. WHERE DO I FIND THE TIME?

Begin by keeping track of how you spend your time for one week. Use the following chart or design your own.

PRESENT TIME SCHEDULE

	MORNING	AFTERNOON	EVENING
SUNDAY			
MONDAY			
TUESDAY			
WEDNESDAY			
THURSDAY			
FRIDAY			
SATURDAY			

ASK YOURSELF:
- What are the things I most enjoy doing? (Circle these items in red ink.)
- What things are required of me on a daily basis? (Circle these items in green ink.)
- What things can I eliminate to make room for new goals? (Circle these items in black ink.)

Continue to next page

2. WHAT DO I WANT?

Ask yourself what you really want in life. What are your lifetime goals? Look at the lists you made in the HOW TO DREAM section, then WRITE DOWN THE GOALS YOU DECIDE YOU WANT TO ACHIEVE.

_____ _____

_____ _____

_____ _____

A. List three long-range goals (five years).
   1. _____
   2. _____
   3. _____

B. List three goals you want to achieve in the next year.
   1. _____
   2. _____
   3. _____

C. List three goals you plan to achieve in the next six months.
   1. _____
   2. _____
   3. _____

D. List three one-month goals.

   _____

   _____

   _____

E. List any goals you want to accomplish next week.

   _____

   _____

   _____

HOW TO PLAN FOR SUCCESS (continued)

3. HOW DO I GET TO WHERE I WANT TO BE?

From your list of goals on page 93, select three goals for detailed planning. Establish an action plan with specific steps and deadlines for attaining each objective. It may be helpful to break the list down into steps or subgoals. Under each, list in detail what needs to be done and by when.

GOAL 1 _____

Start date:

Steps or subgoals:

1.

2.

3.

4.

5.

Finish date:

GOAL 2 _____

Start date:

Steps or subgoals:

1.

2.

3.

4.

5.

Finish date:

GOAL 3 _____

Start date:

Steps or subgoals:

1.

2.

3.

4.

5.

Finish date:

4. What resources do you already have at your disposal to achieve your goals?

A.

B.

C.

What is preventing you from accomplishing your goals?

A.

B.

C.

Can you name some role models who have achieved the goals you want for yourself? What qualities do they possess?

         NAME   QUALITIES

A.   A.

B.   B.

C.   C.

Once you have identified resources that can help you achieve your goals, begin WRITING YOUR GOAL CALENDAR on the next page.

GOAL CALENDARS

Prioritizing your goals according to importance is essential. Short-term goals will lead to long-term success.

INSTRUCTIONS: Use the forms on the next few pages to fill in your goals. These are the things you need to do in order to achieve both short-term and long-term objectives. Fill in the major steps of your plan and assign a completion date for each step.

Cut the forms out or copy them after they have been completed and put them where you will see them each day.

Read them aloud each morning and again each evening.

TODAY'S LIST

ITEM	TO DO	DONE
1.		
2.		
3.		
4.		
5.		

NOTES:

WEEKLY LIST

LIST GOALS SCHEDULED | week 1 | COMPLETED

week 2

week 3

week 4

SIX-MONTH PLAN

(NOTE—You will probably want to design your own forms for your longer-term goals)

January	February	March	April	May	June

ONE-YEAR PLAN

January	February	March	April	May	June

July	August	September	October	November	December

ASK YOURSELF:

1. What obstacles might prevent you from achieving these goals?
2. What activities do you need to do to get started?
3. What activities have you started but not completed?

EIGHT HELPFUL HINTS FOR MANAGING YOUR TIME

1. PLAN:

Look at your weekly goals every day and review your long-term goals on a regular basis (i.e., weekly). Identify specific goals that you want to accomplish today that will help you achieve your long-term goals.

2. CONCENTRATE:

It is difficult to do too many things at once. Make a decision about which project needs your IMMEDIATE attention. Complete one item at a time. The amount of time spent is not what counts, but how effectively the time has been spent. Remember the old saying, ''It's a cinch by the inch, but hard by the yard.''

3. RELAX:

All work and no play leads to unhappiness, inefficiency, boredom, stress, an unbalanced life and feelings of low self-esteem.

Learn to balance your ''career self'' with your ''family self'' and leave time for a ''personal self.'' Balance is the key to personal and career success and to high self-esteem.

Recognize your mental limitations by taking short breaks to provide mental relief. During these periods:

—Do nothing. Relax.
—Change positions. Stand. Walk. Run.
—Try isometric exercises.

Physical activity benefits your health and increases your efficiency.

4. AVOID CONFUSION/UNNECESSARY CLUTTER:

In most cases FEELING organized goes hand in hand with BEING organized.

Categorize your business and/or personal material:
   IMMEDIATE ATTENTION FILE
   IN-PROCESS FILE
   COMPLETED FILE
   READING FILE

An uncluttered desk makes for an uncluttered mind. Remember your priorities.

Never leave your desk at work or home with unattended immediate work to complete. Be organized!

EIGHT HELPFUL HINTS FOR MANAGING YOUR TIME (continued)

5. DO NOT BE AFRAID TO SAY NO:

You do have the right to say NO without feeling guilty. Remember that others also have the right to say NO. Unproductive tasks that do not benefit your objectives will waste your valuable time.

6. DO NOT BE AFRAID TO DELEGATE:

No person is an island. Learning how to delegate can increase your productivity. It will allow more time for those things requiring your personal attention.

REMEMBER: Delegate challenging and rewarding tasks as well as those that you do not care to do. Maximizing and utilizing someone else's strengths will add satisfaction and positive momentum to your environment.

7. OVERCOME PROCRASTINATION:

It is said that if you do anything for a month, it becomes a habit. Overcoming procrastination requires you to form new habits.

Start the day by doing your most unpleasant task. This will free the remainder of the day so you can perform more pleasant tasks.

Attack your most difficult goals regularly. Little by little the end result will become reality. One step forward is better than no step at all.

8. CHECK LIST:

Continue reviewing and reevaluating your priorities, as well as your short-term and long-term goals.

Spend quiet time planning. Fix your mind on what you want.

Review your priority list daily, weekly and monthly. Establish a definite date for beginning and a target date for when you intend to have effected the change or attained the end result.

"YESTERDAY IS A CANCELLED CHECK, TOMORROW IS A PROMISSORY NOTE. TODAY IS READY CASH. . .USE IT!"

Anonymous philosopher

---

*For an excellent book on this subject, order *Personal Time Management* and/or *Time Management and the Telephone* using the information in the back of this book.

SUMMARY

"There is no limit to what you can do, but you need to begin."

When you imagine and visualize what you want and commit your dreams to writing, you will find that taking action is more effective. A focused direction produces focused results. The need to know what you want and how to get there is essential to high self-esteem.

REMEMBER

1. MAKE A LIST OF YOUR DREAMS, THE THINGS YOU WANT TO DO, HAVE AND BE, and a LIST OF YOUR NEEDS. THINK OF THE PEOPLE, FEELINGS AND PLACES THAT YOU WANT AS PART OF YOUR LIFE.

2. SELECT YOUR THREE MOST IMPORTANT GOALS. CHOOSE THE THINGS YOU MOST WANT TO COMMIT TO, ARE MOST EXCITED ABOUT AND WILL GET THE MOST SATISFACTION FROM.

3. REVIEW YOUR GOALS AND ESTIMATE WHEN YOU EXPECT TO COMPLETE THEM: IN ONE WEEK, ONE MONTH, SIX MONTHS, ONE YEAR OR FIVE YEARS?

4. DETERMINE WHAT RESOURCES YOU HAVE AT YOUR DISPOSAL. For example, WHAT ASSETS DO YOU HOLD IN PERSONALITY TRAITS, FRIENDS, FINANCIAL RESOURCES, EDUCATION, TIME AND ENERGY?

5. WHAT CHANGES WILL YOU NEED TO MAKE TO ACHIEVE YOUR GOALS? EDUCATION, MONEY, DISCIPLINE, TIME MANAGEMENT, OVERCOMING PROCRASTINATION?

6. WRITE DOWN WHAT WILL PREVENT YOU FROM REACHING YOUR GOALS.

7. THINK OF SOME ROLE MODELS THAT CAN HELP YOU ACHIEVE YOUR OBJECTIVES.

8. CREATE YOUR GOALS CALENDAR AND PUT IT IN A VISIBLE PLACE THAT YOU SEE DAILY.

"If you do not know where you are going, how will you know when you arrive?"

SECTION SEVEN

TAKE ACTION FOR SUCCESS

SELF-ESTEEM is the most effective antidote to depression, anxiety or stress. It allows one to take ACTION. It is virtually impossible to be active and depressed at the same time. Lack of action can be the cause of depression, which leads to feelings of low self-esteem.

Action also follows thought. Thinking about what you cannot do will often cause you to fail. Positive action, on the other hand, can turn your dreams into reality.

NEVER, NEVER GIVE UP!

INSTRUCTIONS:

1. Each week, keep track of your feelings of self-esteem. Each day put a dot next to the number that most represents how you feel for the day. Try not to think of specifics; recall how you generally felt at the end of that day.

2. At the end of the week connect the dots. It is unrealistic to think each day will be a 10. If you see a slight dip, refer back to your appointment book and reflect on what was happening in your life.

3. In a separate place (i.e., your journal) list what made you feel good when your score was HIGH (6–10) and what made you feel not so good when your score was LOW (5–0). Review your comments regularly to see if there are recurring patterns.

	SUNDAY	MONDAY	TUESDAY	WEDNESDAY	THURSDAY	FRIDAY	SATURDAY
HIGH 10							
9							
8							
7							
6							
5							
4							
3							
2							
1							
LOW 0							

NEVER, NEVER GIVE UP (continued)

4. Review your list of HIGHs and LOWs and then write in the form below
WHAT YOU WANT TO CHANGE, as well as STEPS YOU NEED TO TAKE
and WHEN THEY WILL BE TAKEN.

THINGS I WANT TO CHANGE	STEPS I WILL TAKE	WHEN
e.g., Expand my personal contacts.	Take dancing lessons at the recreation center.	By next Friday.

(You may wish to design your own form)

5. Review THE RESOURCES THAT YOU HAVE FOR FEELING GOOD ABOUT
   YOURSELF. Think in terms of INTERNAL RESOURCES and your MARKETABLE
   STRENGTHS (Section Four). Think in terms of EXTERNAL RESOURCES,
   those that serve as your SUPPORT SYSTEM (identified in Section Three).

List your EXTERNAL RESOURCES below and put an ''E.'' Then list your
INTERNAL RESOURCES and put an ''I.''

INDICATE HOW OFTEN YOU FELT GOOD OR BAD next to these Internal or
External Resources:
''D'' FOR DAILY
''W'' FOR WEEKLY
''M'' MONTHLY

For example: Chairing a Committee would be ''E & I'', ''M''
Jogging might be ''I'' ''D''

LIST EXTERNAL AND INTERNAL RESOURCES	E OR I	DAILY-D WEEKLY-W MONTHLY-M
1.		
2.		
3.		
4.		
5.		
6.		
7.		
8.		

How balanced are you? If most of your self-esteem is coming from ''External
Resources,'' you may need to reevaluate how much you depend on others. Try
relying on yourself for opinions and compliments, and put more energy into
complimenting others.

TO DO LIST

DAILY REMINDER

Repeat aloud: "TODAY I CHOOSE TO HAVE A GOOD DAY. I WILL CONSCIOUSLY LOOK FOR THE GOOD IN OTHERS AND COMMUNICATE CONFIDENCE TO MYSELF AND OTHERS."

LIST:

TODAY I FOUND MYSELF THINKING/FEELING THE FOLLOWING POSITIVE THINGS: (ATTITUDES) _____

_____

_____

TODAY I TOOK THE TIME TO DO THE FOLLOWING JUST FOR ME: _____

_____

_____

TODAY I IMPROVED MY MIND BY: _____

_____

_____

TODAY I TOOK TIME TO IMPROVE MY PHYSICAL SELF BY: _____

_____

_____

TODAY I MADE SOMEONE ELSE FEEL GOOD BY: _____

_____

_____

SUMMARY

The key to personal and career success is believing in yourself. Self-esteem is a state of mind and an attitude that comes from within. By taking responsibility for your own choices and decisions, you have the power to control your thoughts, your actions and your level of self-esteem.

Writing down your thoughts will help develop a sense of closeness and an awareness of your unique strengths. This can provide you with a framework from which to plan your future and achieve your dreams. By starting now to make changes, you can change your life. You can adapt, grow and evolve by changing your perceptions and by thinking your actions will produce results at work and at home. A sense of WHOLENESS, FOCUS and BALANCE will follow.

ACTION AND SELF-ESTEEM GO HAND IN HAND BECAUSE SELF-ESTEEM IS THE BRIDGE BETWEEN WHO YOU ARE AND WHAT YOU DO.

''I challenge you to double the amount of energy and enthusiasm you are putting into your life. I guarantee you will triple your feelings of self-esteem, happiness and success.''

C. Palladino

''Finish every day and be done with it. You have done what you could. Some blunders and absurdities no doubt crept in; forget them as soon as you can.

Tomorrow is a new day; begin it well and serenely and with too high a spirit to be encumbered with your old nonsense.

This day is all that is good and fair. It is too dear, with its hopes and invitations, to waste a moment on yesterday.''

Ralph Waldo Emerson

P A R T

III

SUMMARY AND
APPENDIX

YOUR SELF-ESTEEM ACTION PLAN:

I PLAN TO:

☐ **1. TAKE TIME TO OVERCOME MY FEARS.**
—*Visualize, Verbalize, Practice and Experience*

☐ **2. CREATE A POSITIVE BELIEF SYSTEM FOR MYSELF AT WORK and AT HOME.**
—*Evaluate my attitude. It affects everything I do and how I relate to others.*

☐ **3. FOCUS IN ON MY MARKETABLE STRENGTHS.**
—*Who Am I Today? Where Am I Going?*
—*Concentrate on my strengths, special talents, aptitudes, hobbies, education, work and relationships.*
—*My facial expressions, tone of voice, posture, stance and gestures convey who I am.*

☐ **4. TAKE TIME TO DREAM and PLAN.**
—*Set daily, weekly, monthly goals, develop a road map of activities and plan for how to get from where I am to where I want to go.*

☐ **5. DO IT NOW. TAKE ACTION!**
—*Strengthen my mind, seek new challenges and responsibilities and take advantage of what I know.*

FINAL THOUGHTS

We all have greater challenges today than ever before. Our jobs, our family pressures and the need to balance both in an imbalanced society make things difficult. Our society is struggling with the influence of drugs and alcoholism, increased crime and violence, teen pregnancy, the impact of welfare dependency and child and spousal abuse, to name just a few problems. The truth is, however, that **WE CAN MAKE A DIFFERENCE. WE ARE ALL PARTNERS IN THIS JOURNEY AND CAN ALL SERVE AS ROLE MODELS.**

Please take the ideas, exercises and suggested readings in this book and share them with your co-workers, friends and family. Sharing these ideas may remind you that what you value and believe is important. Richness and joy comes not only from helping yourself, but from helping others as well.

Whitney Houston's beautiful song says it all. *The Greatest Love of All* is learning to love yourself. "Let the children lead the way and show them the beauty they possess inside. Give them a sense of pride and let their laughter remind us of how we used to be."

Good luck in your journey!

APPENDIX

RECOMMENDED BOOKS FROM OTHER PUBLISHERS INCLUDE:

Self-Esteem

CELEBRATE YOUR SELF: MAKING LIFE WORK FOR YOU by Dorothy Briggs

HOW DO I LOVE ME? by Helen M. Johnson

THE PSYCHOLOGY OF SELF-ESTEEM
HOW TO RAISE YOUR SELF-ESTEEM by Nathaniel Branden

MAKING CONTACT SELF-ESTEEM by Virginia Satir

WOMEN AND SELF-ESTEEM by Linda T. Sanford and Mary Ellen Donovan

BUILDING SELF-ESTEEM by Robert Reasoner

Risk Change and Overcome Fear

WHEN SMART PEOPLE FAIL by Carole Hyatt and Linda Gottlieb

TRANSITIONS by William Bridges

ASSERTING YOURSELF by Sharon and Gordon Bower

LOVE IS LETTING GO OF FEAR by Gerald Jampolsky and Jack O'Keeler

Create a Positive Belief System

PSYCHO-CYBERNETICS by Maxwell Maltz

THINK AND GROW RICH by Napolean Hill

THANK GOD IT'S MONDAY by Pierre Mornell

STRESS WITHOUT DISTRESS by Hans Selye

SEEDS OF GREATNESS by Denis Waitley

RECOMMENDED BOOKS FROM OTHER PUBLISHERS INCLUDE: (continued)

Identify Your Marketable Career Strengths

THE JOY OF WORKING by Denis Waitley

WORK WITH PASSION: HOW TO DO WHAT YOU LOVE FOR A LIVING by Nancy Anderson

FOCUS: A PROFESSIONAL DEVELOPMENT PROGRAM by Connie Palladino

WHAT COLOR IS YOUR PARACHUTE? by Richard Bolles

TAKE THIS JOB AND LOVE IT by Dennis Jaffee and Cynthia Scott

DO WHAT YOU LOVE, THE MONEY WILL FOLLOW by Marsha Sinetar

Take the Time to Dream

WISHCRAFT: HOW TO GET WHAT YOU REALLY WANT by Barbara Sher

CREATIVE VISUALIZATION by Shakti Gawain

Goal Setting

ALL ABOUT GOALS by Jack Addington

HOW TO GET CONTROL OF YOUR TIME AND YOUR LIFE by Alan Lakein

HOW TO PUT MORE TIME IN YOUR LIFE by Dru Scott

Action

COMFORT ZONES: A PRACTICAL GUIDE FOR RETIREMENT by Elwood Chapman

NOTES

NOTES

NOTES

NOTES